中国思想文化术语多语种对外翻译
标准化建设项目成果
CHINESE THINKING AND CULTURE
MULTILINGUAL TERMINOLOGY DATABASE

中华源·河南故事
CHINESE CIVILIZATION
Stories from Henan

淮河文化
THE HUAIHE RIVER CULTURE

河南省人民政府外事办公室　编

河南大学出版社
HENAN UNIVERSITY PRESS
·郑州·

图书在版编目（CIP）数据

中华源·河南故事．淮河文化：汉英对照 / 河南省人民政府外事办公室编 . -- 郑州：河南大学出版社，2022.6

ISBN 978-7-5649-5196-2

Ⅰ．①中… Ⅱ．①河… Ⅲ．①地方文化－河南－通俗读物－汉、英②淮河流域－地方文化－通俗读物－汉、英 Ⅳ．① G127.61-49

中国版本图书馆 CIP 数据核字（2022）第 110905 号

淮河文化
HUAI HE WENHUA

责任编辑	张雪彩
责任校对	林方丽
封面设计	翟淼淼
版式设计	高枫叶
出版发行	河南大学出版社
	地址：郑州市郑东新区商务外环中华大厦2401号　邮编：450046
	电话：0371-86059701（营销部）
	0371-86059750（高等教育与职业教育分公司）
	网址：hupress.henu.edu.cn
排　　版	河南大学出版社设计排版部
印　　刷	河南博雅彩印有限公司
版　　次	2022年6月第1版　　　印　次　2022年6月第1次印刷
开　　本	710 mm×1010 mm　1/16　　印　张　15
字　　数	240千字　　　　　　　　定　价　75.00元

版权所有，侵权必究
本书如有印装质量问题，请与河南大学出版社营销部联系调换。

"中华源·河南故事"系列丛书编委会

顾　　问	黄友义　杨　平　范大祺
主　　任	梁杰一
副 主 任	卞　科　陈　岩　陈志伟　刁玉华　方启雄　韩国河 惠　康　焦开举　介晓磊　孔留安　李冰冰　李　俊 刘炯天　李向前　李　镇　梁留科　刘金锋　马萧林 牛书成　牛卫国　屈凌波　屈鹏飞　史永庆　田　凯 万正峰　王建修　王清义　王自文　许二平　杨建伟 杨玮斌　俞海洛　张改平　张俊峰　张明超　张松文 赵卫东
主　　编	梁杰一
副 主 编	李冰冰
编　　委	陈国良　陈　玮　丁　锐　高　阳　徐恒振　郑延保 孙立英　郭　远

中华源·河南故事·淮河文化

主　　编	李　俊
副 主 编	金荣权　蔡满园（英文）
中文撰稿	张义明　郭德华　孙　炜　蔡亚玲
英文译者	余永锋　曹万忠　宣军磊　王辰玲
英文审校	[英] Nicholas Richard

The Editorial Committee
Chinese Civilization
Stories from Henan

Consultants	Huang Youyi Yang Ping Fan Daqi
Director	Liang Jieyi
Deputy Directors	Bian Ke Chen Yan Chen Zhiwei Diao Yuhua
	Fang Qixiong Han Guohe Hui Kang Jiao Kaiju
	Jie Xiaolei Kong Liu'an Li Bingbing Li Jun
	Liu Jiongtian Li Xiangqian Li Zhen Liang Liuke
	Liu Jinfeng Ma Xiaolin Niu Shucheng Niu Weiguo
	Qu Lingbo Qu Pengfei Shi Yongqing Tian Kai
	Wan Zhengfeng Wang Jianxiu Wang Qingyi Wang Ziwen
	Xu Erping Yang Jianwei Yang Weibin Yu Hailuo
	Zhang Gaiping Zhang Junfeng Zhang Mingchao
	Zhang Songwen Zhao Weidong
Chief Editor	Liang Jieyi
Deputy Chief Editor	Li Bingbing
Editors	Chen Guoliang Chen Wei Ding Rui Gao Yang
	Xu Hengzhen Zheng Yanbao Sun Liying Guo Yuan

Chinese Civilization
Stories from Henan
The Huaihe River Culture

Editor-in-Chief	Li Jun
Associate Editors-in-Chief	Jin Rongquan Cai Manyuan (English)
Writers	Zhang Yiming Guo Dehua Sun Wei Cai Yaling
Translators	Yu Yongfeng Cao Wanzhong Xuan Junlei
	Wang Chenling
Translation Proofreader	Nicholas Richard (UK)

总　序

中国是世界四大文明古国之一，也是世界上唯一的古代文明传统未曾中断的国家。河南省地处中国中东部，是中华文明和中华民族的重要发祥地，在中国五千年的文明史上，河南作为国家政治、经济、文化的中心就长达三千多年。从某种意义上讲，一部河南史就是半部中国史。这里是中华人文始祖黄帝的故乡，是古丝绸之路的东方起点，是少林功夫和陈氏太极的发源地，这里创建了中国历史上最早的都城，镌刻了中国最古老的文字，诞生了中国最初的商业文明。

伴随着新时代的荣光，河南经济社会发展迅速，人民生活水平显著提升，这是河南人民自力更生、艰苦奋斗的历史结果，也是对外开放带来的益处。河南经济社会的发展、人民生活方式的改变都植根于深层次的文化积淀。为了让世界更多地了解河南，让河南更好地走向世界，2018年以来，河南省人民政府外事办公室认真研析了这片古老土地上的历史文化资源和时代风貌，组织各领域权威专家学者，编译了"中华源·河南故事"中外文系列丛书，选取黄河文化、河洛文化、老子、庄子、黄帝、少林功夫、太极拳、中医、汉字、丝绸之路、古都、农业、大运河、文物、陶瓷、青铜器、手工艺、书法、杂技、豫菜、豫剧、脱贫攻坚、空中丝绸之路、航空城、南水北调、中原粮谷、红旗渠、焦裕禄等多个主题，力图以故事的方式向世界展现一个立体、全面、真实的河南。

当今世界，人类文明无论是在物质还是在精神方面都取得了巨大进步，特别是物质的极大丰富，这在古代世界是完全不能想象的。同时，当代人类也面临着许多突出的难题，比如，贫富差距持续扩大，物欲追求奢华无度，个人主义恶性膨胀，社会诚信不断消减，伦理道德每况愈下，人与自然关系日趋紧张，等等。要解决这些难题，不仅需要运用人类今天的智慧和力量，而且需要运用人类历史上积累和储存的智慧和力量。河南历史文化底蕴深厚、包容性强，在今天仍极具现实意义。中原文化蕴含的思想智慧有助于修身养性，推动人类社会进步发展，焦裕禄精神、红旗渠精神所体现的为民爱民、艰苦奋斗的价值取向是构建人类命运共同体的力量源泉。我们期待与读者们一起从河南故事中汲取更多的智慧和力量，共同创造更加美好的未来。

Series Foreword

China is one of the four ancient civilizations in the world, and is also the only country in the world where the ancient civilization has not been interrupted. Located in east-central China, Henan Province is an important cradle for the Chinese nation and Chinese civilization. In the course of the five thousand years of Chinese history, for more than three thousand years it served as the political, economic and cultural center of the country and therefore, as generally accepted, represents half of the history of China. Henan is the native place of Yellow Emperor, the cradle of Chinese culture, the starting point of the ancient Silk Road in the east, and the birthplace of Shaolin Kungfu and Chen-style Taijiquan—typical examples of the world-renowned Chinese martial arts. It was here that the earliest capital city in China was founded, the oldest Chinese characters engraved, and the earliest commerce took shape.

In the new era, Henan has witnessed rapid growth in its economy and remarkable improvement of people's living conditions owing to the national reform and opening-up policy and unremitting endeavors of the people. Modern economic achievements and social development as well as the changes of way of life could be traced back to its traditional values and cultural heritages. To enable people from other countries to understand Henan, and let the Province integrate more efficiently into the world development, the Foreign Affairs Office of the People's Government of Henan Province has organized teams of authoritative experts and scholars in relevant fields to compile this *Chinese Civilization: Stories from Henan* in Chinese and foreign languages since 2018 by crystallizing the excellence of traditions and outstanding features of modern development. The book series include *The Yellow River Culture*, *Heluo Culture*, *Laozi*, *Zhuangzi*, *The Yellow Emperor*, *Shaolin Kungfu*, *Taijiquan*, *Traditional Chinese Medicine*,

Chinese Characters, *The Silk Road*, *Ancient Chinese Capitals*, *Feeding the People—Agriculture*, *The Grand Canal*, *Cultural Heritage*, *Ceramic*, *Bronze*, *Handicraft Art*, *Calligraphy*, *Acrobatics*, *Henan Cuisine*, *Henan Opera*, *Poverty Alleviation*, *Silk Road in the Air*, *Zhengzhou—An Aviation City*, *South-to-North Water Diversion*, *Grain of the Central Plains*, *Man-Made River—Hongqiqu Canal*, *A Model Official—Jiao Yulu*, etc., presenting a panoramic picture of the Province.

In today's world, human civilization has made great progress in both material accumulation and ethical advancement, and the great abundance of materials today, especially, is beyond the imagination of the ancient people. At the same time, however, modern people are also confronted with a lot of problems, such as the widening gap between the rich and the poor, the indulgence in pursuit of luxury and extravagance, the undesirable extension of individualism, the decline of social integrity, and the increasingly tense relationship between man and nature. To solve the problems, we need to draw on the wisdom and powers developed today as well as those accumulated in the past. Henan is endowed with rich historical and cultural heritages characterized by its inclusiveness, and such heritages remain significant today. The intelligence and wisdom in Henan culture are conducive to self-cultivation and to the promotion of social development. The spirit of serving the people and relentless struggle, as embodied in Jiao Yulu and the man-made river—Hongqiqu Canal provides source of strength for building a community with a shared future for mankind. It is our hope that wisdom and strength from Henan stories could lead us to a shared brilliant future.

前　言

千里长淮万卷书，四季浪花唱古今。相传宇宙之始，天地一片混沌。历经一万八千余年，一个叫盘古的巨人，拿起神斧，劈向四方。自此，天空高远，大地辽阔。盘古因开天劈地，成为中华民族崇拜的英雄。盘古的故事，发生在秦岭东部余脉，今桐柏山境内。斗转星移，自桐柏山始，一条淮河自西向东蜿蜒流淌，见证了岁月千年，也孕育出了淮河流域灿烂的文化，史称"淮河文化"。

淮河文化交融汇集的品格构成了中华文化的重要支柱。与黄河流域"政教为主"、长江流域"经济特色"鲜明的情况相比，淮河流域"思想文化"的特色十分突出。在漫长的历史岁月中，淮河流域孕育出了以老子、庄子、管子、颜回等为代表的先哲圣贤，以及"三曹父子""竹林七贤"等文学艺术巨擘。我国的孔孟儒家学说，墨家学派，韩非、李斯的法家学派，都是在淮河流域创立的。从文化史角度溯源，淮河文化源于长江流域的楚文化，兴盛于淮河流域的宋、明文化。在这里，北方的中原文化、东部的齐鲁文化、东南的吴越文化和南方的楚文化从先秦以来就相互交汇、碰撞，逐渐融合，从而成为中华民族传统文化的有机组成部分。而多种文化因子的并存，也铸就了这一地区文化的独特魅力。

淮河流域是我国稻作农业的重要起源地，为中国后代稻作农业的发展奠定了基础；淮河流域龟灵崇拜成为我国占卜文化的源头，这种古老的龟灵崇拜占卜方式直接开启了我国传统的八卦文化和易经文化，同时也启发了商人用钻灼牛骨、龟甲定吉凶的方法；淮河流域是我国史前文字重要的起源地之一。

淮河流域拥有丰富的历史文化遗产。这里有盘古开天劈地之地——淮河源头桐柏山；有人们为追忆"三皇五帝"之首天皇伏羲氏的功绩而建造的伏羲陵庙；有鲧和大禹父子治水的美丽传说以及有关历史、政治、文化名人的历史典故。另外，以根亲文化为代表的淮河移民文化、以淮河上的"东方芭蕾"——花鼓灯为代表的淮河民歌民俗文化、以"信阳毛尖"为代表的信阳饮食文化都让淮河文化"中原文化之中原"的称号实至名归。

Preface

The Huaihe River, a thousand miles long, runs endlessly eastward; story in volumes, past and present, witnesses the Chinese vicissitude. The universe in the beginning, was utterly in chaotic. A giant named Pan Gu, woke from his 18,000-years' lethargy and with his magic axe, made the epoch-making myth of the creation of heaven and earth. Since then, the sky hangs high and the earth, vast. And Pan Gu was venerated as the national hero of Chinese nation. The legend of Pan Gu occurred in the eastern ranges of the Qinling Mountains within the present territory of the Tongbai Mountain. Running out of the Tongbai Mountain and wending her way east, the Huaihe River witnessed time and tide for thousands of years and nurtured the splendid culture in the Huaihe River Basin, historically known as "the Huaihe River Culture".

The Huaihe River Culture, known for her quality of integration and convergence, is an important pillar of Chinese culture. It highlights ideological and cultural factors, instead of giving priority to those political and religious ones in the Yellow River Basin or economic ones in the Yangtze River Basin. In the long history of human development, the Huaihe River Basin gave birth to eminent sages such as Lao Tseu, Chuang Tzu, Guan Zhong and Yan Hui as well as literary giants such as the three Cao (Cao Cao, Cao Pi and Cao Zhi in the late Eastern Han Dynasty) and the Seven Sages of the Metaphysics (seven literary figures in the Wei and Jin dynasties). Those traditional theories of the nation such as Confucianism proposed by Confucius and Mencius, legalism proposed by Han Fei and Li Si, as well as Mohism were all established here in the Huaihe River Basin. When tracing the origin from the perspective of the cultural history, the Huaihe River Culture originated from the Chu Culture in the Yangtze River Basin and flourished during the Song and Ming dynasties in the Huaihe River Basin. Starting as early in the Pre-Qin period, different cultures, including the Central Plains Culture in the north, the Qi and Lu Culture (culture of Qi Kingdom and Lu Kingdom in the Pre-Qin period) in the east, the Wu and Yue Culture in the southeast, and the Chu Culture in the south, have converged and collided with each other gradually since the Pre-Qin period, becoming organic components of Chinese traditional culture. This juxtaposition of multi-cultural factors bestowed the traditions of the region with unique charm.

As an important region where paddy agriculture originated, rice farming in the Huaihe River Basin laid the foundation for the development of rice farming for descendants in China. Tortoise worship is the origin of Divination Culture in China, which directly relates to the traditional Eight Diagram Culture and I-ching Culture of the nation, and at the same time inspires people in the Shang Dynasty to take the advantage of articles such as scorched and drilled bovine bone or tortoise shell to predict whether the time would be auspicious or vice versa. The Huaihe River Basin is also the cradle of prehistoric paleography.

The Huaihe River Basin boasts of her diversified historical and culture relics and legacies. The Tongbai Mountain, where the Huaihe River springs from, is said to be the site where Pan Gu's epoch-making myth happened; the Fu Xi Temple is located here to commemorate his admirable service as the leading figure among the Three Sovereigns and Five Emperors in ancient China. There are beautiful legends about Gun and Da Yu's (a father and son pair in ancient China) taming of the flood. Furthermore, the Huaihe River Basin is also renowned for her Huaihe emigrant culture represented by ancestral roots seeking culture, Huaihe folk songs and customs represented by the so-called Eastern ballet on the Huaihe River—Huadu Dance, and Xinyang dietary culture represented by the Xinyang Maojian Tea. All these factors give the Huaihe River Culture the well-deserved title of the "Central Plains of Central Plains Culture".

目 录　　　　　　　　　　　　　　Contents

第一章　历史篇：淮河与华夏文明　　　　　　　　001
　　一、淮河流域上古的独特文化　　　　　　　　002
　　二、淮河流域龟灵崇拜与占卜文化　　　　　　006
　　三、淮河流域与汉字的发展　　　　　　　　　010
　　四、淮河流域是我国稻作农业的重要起源地　　014
　　五、淮河流域与中华民族的形成　　　　　　　018

Chapter 1　History: The Huaihe River and Chinese Culture　　001
　　I. Unique Palaeoid Culture in the Huaihe River Basin　　003
　　II. Tortoise Worship and Divination Culture in the Huaihe River Basin　　007
　　III. The Huaihe River Basin and the Evolution of Chinese Characters　　011
　　IV. The Huaihe River Basin—An Important Cradle of Chinese Paddy Agriculture　　015
　　V. The Huaihe River Basin and the Formation of Chinese Nation　　019

第二章　根亲篇：淮河流域的移民与根亲文化　　025
　　一、光州固始向福建的移民　　　　　　　　　026
　　二、固始移民由福建向台湾和海外的播迁　　　034
　　三、姓氏寻根到中原　　　　　　　　　　　　044

Chapter 2　Root Seeking: The Emigrant and Root Seeking Culture in the Huaihe River Basin　　025
　　I. The Emigration from Gushi Guangzhou to Fujian Province　　027
　　II. Migration of Gushi Migrants from Fujian to Taiwan and Overseas　　035
　　III. Central Plains Ancestral Root Seeking of Different Families　　045

第三章　水利篇：淮河水利文化　　　055
　　一、大禹治淮　　　056
　　二、孙叔敖治淮　　　064
　　三、一定要把淮河修好　　　068

Chapter 3　Water Conservation: Water Conservation Culture of the Huaihe River　　　055
　　I. Yu the Great's Taming of the Flood　　　057
　　II. Sunshu Ao's Fixing of the Huaihe River　　　065
　　III. Resolutely to Tame the Huaihe River　　　069

第四章　饮食篇：信阳茶和信阳菜　　　079
　　一、信阳茶：信阳毛尖　　　080
　　二、信阳菜：豫楚风味　　　098

Chapter 4　Diets: Xinyang Tea and Cuisine　　　079
　　I. Xinyang Green Tea: Xinyang Maojian　　　081
　　II. Xinyang Cuisine: A Blending of the Flavors Both of Henan and
　　　　Hubei Cuisines　　　099

第五章　民俗篇：淮河民俗文化　　　109
　　一、物质生活民俗　　　110
　　二、社会生活民俗　　　124
　　三、精神生活民俗　　　132
　　四、新民俗　　　138

Chapter 5 Folk Customs: Folk Cultures Along the Huaihe River	109
I. Folk Customs on Material Life	111
II. Folk Customs on Social Life	125
III. Folk Customs on Spiritual Life	133
IV. New Folk Customs	139
第六章 音乐篇：淮河民间音乐文化	143
一、唱着过的岁月：民间歌曲	144
二、淮水"三花"：民间舞蹈	152
三、农耕文明的音声场：民间戏剧	162
Chapter 6 Music: Folk Music Culture Along the Huaihe River	143
I. Years Full of Songs: Folk Songs	145
II. "Three Flowers" Along the Huaihe River: Folk Dances	153
III. Sounds of Agricultural Civilization: Folk Operas	163
第七章 典故篇：信阳典故	171
Chapter 7 Historic Tales: Historic Tales in Xinyang	171
第八章 前景篇：淮河与"一带一路"	187
一、国家战略：淮河生态经济带	188
二、淮河干流港：淮滨港	204
三、淮河支流港：周口港	208
四、淮河边走出的外交官：荀皓东	214

Chapter 8   Prospects: The Huaihe River and the Belt and Road Initiative   187
    I. National Strategy: The Ecological Economic Belt Along the Huaihe River   189
    II. The Huaibin Harbour: A Mainstream Harbor of the Huaihe River   205
    III. Zhoukou Harbour: A Branch Harbour of the Huaihe River   209
    IV. Gou Haodong: A Diplomat Having Grown Up by the Huaihe River   215

结　语   220
Conclusion   221

附录：中国历史年代简表   222
Appendix: A Brief Chronology of Chinese History   222

第一章

历史篇：淮河与华夏文明

Chapter 1

History: The Huaihe River and Chinese Culture

淮河是我国主要河流之一，地处南北过渡带，土地肥沃、气候湿润、植被丰富，早在旧石器和新石器时代就有先民们在这里繁衍、生息，并创造了辉煌的史前文明。

随着考古工作的不断深入和越来越多的史前文化遗址的发现，证明在史前时代，淮河流域不仅有着灿烂的史前文明，而且有着自己独立发展的文化体系，这种文化体系一方面在持续吸纳周边文化精华的基础上得到充实、发展，同时又对其他文化序列产生重大影响。

一、淮河流域上古的独特文化

从考古发现来看，早在旧石器时代的不同时期，淮河流域就有多支先民在此生息。在新石器时代，由于淮河流域特殊的地理位置和温润的气候更适合人类居住以及文化上的交流，这一地区的文化得到快速发展。淮河流域上游有距今约9000到7000年的裴李岗—贾湖文化；中游有距今8000到7700年的小山口、侯家寨、双墩文化；下游在距今8500到5000年之间分别出现了顺山集文化、北辛文化、青莲岗文化和大汶口文化等。这些文化类型无论在时代久远方面还是在文明程度上都不亚于黄河流域的大地湾文化、仰韶文化，长江流域的彭头山文化、河姆渡文化、大溪文化、马家浜文化、崧泽—良渚文化以及屈家岭文化。

要确立淮河流域史前文化的独立性和历史地位，首先需要弄清楚这一区域史前文化的主源文化和其后续的继承与发展。研究表明，史前时期淮河流域的主源文化是距今9000到7000年之间产生于淮河上游的贾湖文化。距今约7000年前，贾湖人沿淮河两岸渐次向东迁徙，最终到达苏北和鲁中南地区，并与当地土著居民相融合，首先影响到北辛文化，然后又生成了大汶口文化。于是，贾湖人的龟灵崇拜、随葬獐牙器和绿松石饰以及猪牙器的习俗，贾湖人使用的石磨盘、齿刃石镰和大石铲等经典农业用具，贾湖人的陶锉，都随贾湖人的东迁被传播至淮河中下游。

As one of the major rivers of China, the Huaihe River is located in the transitional zone between the north and south, prestigious for her fertile soil, moist climate and lush vegetation. Our ancestors lived and thrived here as early in the Palaeolithic and Neolithic ages, and created the magnificent prehistoric civilization.

With the constant deepening of archaeological excavation and the increasing discovery of those prehistoric relics, it is evident that there was not only splendid prehistoric civilization, but also an independent cultural system in the Huaihe River Basin, constantly being enriched and developed by absorbing the essence of the cultures in the neighboring regions, while at the same time having a great impact on those cultures.

I. Unique Palaeoid Culture in the Huaihe River Basin

According to the archaeological discovery, ancestors of different tribes lived and thrived in the Huaihe River Basin as early in different periods of the Palaeolithic Age, while in the Neolithic Age, the culture in this region developed rapidly due to its unique geographical location and moist climate. There was the Peiligang-Jiahu Culture about 9,000 to 7,000 years ago in the upper reaches of the Huaihe River Basin; the Xiaoshankou, Houjiazhai and Shuangdun cultures 8,000 to 7,700 years ago in the middle reaches and the Shunshanji Culture, Beixin Culture, Qingliangang Culture and Dawenkou Culture 8,500 to 5,000 years ago in the lower reaches. All these cultures, either taking time or level of civilization into consideration, were highly advanced in comparison with those in the Yellow River Basin such as the Dadiwan Culture and Yangshao Culture, and those in the Yangtze River Basin such as the Pengtoushan Culture, Hemudu Culture, Daxi Culture, Majiabang Culture, Songze-Liangzhu Culture and Qujialing Culture.

To establish the notion of the independence and historical status of the prehistoric culture in the Huaihe River Basin, it is necessary to make it clear about the main source culture and her subsequent inheritance and development of the prehistoric culture in this region. Research shows that the main source culture in the prehistoric Huaihe River Basin is the Jiahu Culture, which originated in the upper reaches between 9,000 to 7,000 years ago. The Jiahu people, about 7,000

由此可推测，北辛—大汶口文化的主要源头即贾湖文化，而此后的山东龙山文化又是继承大汶口文化发展而来，所以贾湖文化作为主源文化影响了整个淮河流域的史前文化。

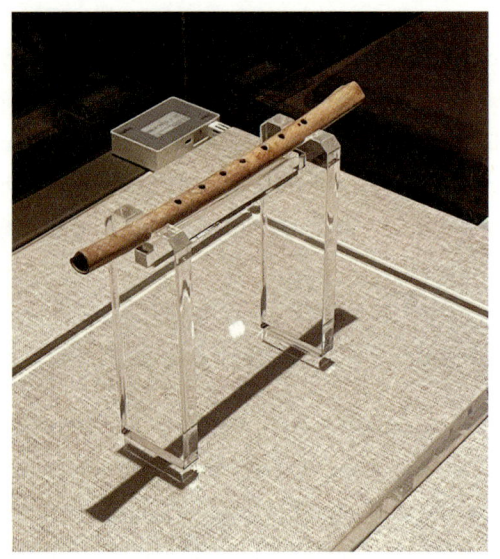

在距今 8000 年的淮河上游贾湖遗址出土的骨笛（信阳学院冯春晓摄影）
Bone Flute Unearthed in the Jiahu Site Dating Back to 8,000 Years Ago in the Upper Reaches of the Huaihe River (Photography by Feng Chunxiao, Xinyang University)

years ago, started their gradual eastward migration along the banks of the Huaihe River, and eventually reached and merged with the local aborigines in the north of Jiangsu Province and south-central Shandong Province. The Jiahu Culture, first of all, influenced the Beixin Culture and then generated the Dawenkou Culture. Consequently, customs such as tortoise worship and the use of roe tooth vessels, pig tooth vessels and turquoise ornaments as burial accessories, and those daily used agricultural implements such as millstones, notched blade sickles, large stone spades and pottery files of the Jiahu people, were brought and dispersed to the middle and lower reaches of the Huaihe River in the process of their eastward migration. Therefore, it can be inferred that the main source of the Beixin-Dawenkou Culture is the Jiahu Culture, and the succeeding Longshan Culture in Shandong Province is inherited from the Dawenkou Culture, making the Jiahu Culture the main source culture and influencing the whole prehistoric culture of the Huaihe River Basin.

二、淮河流域龟灵崇拜与占卜文化

龟灵崇拜是我国史前文化中一个独特的文化现象。在贾湖遗址中出土了大量的龟甲，这些龟甲大多都是随葬之物，在贾湖人的墓地中有 23 座墓葬中有随葬的龟甲，多者有 8 龟，少者 1 龟。龟甲的数量多少应与死者的地位、身份有关，其用途或反映出贾湖人当时的某种宗教习俗，很可能是贾湖人所发明的早期卜筮。随着贾湖人的东迁，这种龟灵崇拜习俗也被带到了海岱地区，为北辛—大汶口—龙山文化所继承。根据现有的考古材料来看，在山东泰安大汶口、兖州王因，江苏邳县刘林和大墩子等墓地也都有随葬龟甲的现象，一些龟壳内装有石子或骨针等物件。从贾湖文化到大汶口文化，这种一脉相承的龟灵崇拜现象，能够跨越千里之遥，延续数千年之久，绝对不是简单的习俗，而是能够反映一种深刻信仰的文化现象。如果说贾湖人和大汶口文化中的龟灵崇拜现象只是我国龟卜文化萌芽的话，那么到了凌家滩文化时期则发展、演变为比较成熟的龟卜文化。在安徽含山县铜闸镇凌家滩 07M23 墓中，墓主人腰部正中位置放有一件玉龟及两件玉龟状器物，玉龟背甲尾端有两个对钻的小圆孔，3 件玉龟（玉龟状器物）腹内放置共 5 件玉签。与玉龟同时出土并叠压在一起的还有一块玉版，玉版正面有两个大小相套的圆圈，内外圆之间有八条直线将图案分为八等份。研究者认为这种图案当为我国的原始八卦。

凌家滩出土的器物反映出淮河流域先民太阳崇拜、鸟崇拜和龟灵崇拜的倾向，其主源是东夷部族的大汶口文化。在大汶口文化时期，东夷人的一支从山东迁往安徽江淮一带，吸纳了当地的土著文化，同时也融合了周边的史前文化，从而形成了独具特色的文化类型。凌家滩人将贾湖—大汶口文化中的龟灵崇拜进一步发展：龟灵崇拜的材料由原来的自然生物之龟甲变成了玉质龟甲，龟壳内所放置的石子、骨针等简易之物

II. Tortoise Worship and Divination Culture in the Huaihe River Basin

Tortoise worship is a unique cultural phenomenon in Chinese prehistoric culture. A large number of tortoise shells used as burial accessories have been unearthed in the Jiahu site. The number of tombs with tortoise shells in the site amounted to 23 with the maximum of 8 tortoise shells and the minimum of one in each tomb. The number of tortoise shells should be related to the status and identity of the deceased, which might reflect a certain religious custom of the Jiahu people at that time, and was probably an early custom of the Jiahu people. With the eastward migration of the Jiahu people, this custom of tortoise worship was also brought to the Haidai Region (the region around the Taishan Mountain and the Yimeng Mountains area), and later was inherited by the Beixin-Dawenkou-Longshan Culture. According to the existing archaeological data, tortoise shells, including stones and spicula etc. within some of the shells, also appeared as burial accessories in the tombs of Dawenkou in Tai'an and Wangyin in Yanzhou, Shandong Province, and Liulin and Dadunzi in Pi County, Jiangsu Province. From the Jiahu Culture to the Dawenkou Culture, the custom of tortoise worship, which spanned thousands of miles and lasted for thousands of years, is definitely not a simple custom, but a cultural phenomenon reflective of a metaphysical belief system. If the tortoise worship in the Jiahu Culture and the Dawenkou Culture represented only the embryonic stage of Chinese tortoise divination culture, then it developed and evolved into a relatively mature one in the Lingjiatan Culture period. In the number 07M23 tomb of Lingjiatan Village, Tongzha Town, Hanshan County, Anhui Province, a jade tortoise and two jade tortoise-like implements were put right in the middle of the tomb owner's waist, and there laid two symmetrical small round holes at the tail end of the tortoise shell, and 5 pieces of jade fortune-sticks in the enterocoelia of the 3 jade tortoises or the jade tortoise-like implements respectively. Stacked together with the jade tortoise, there was a jade plate with two circles of identical size, and on the front side were eight straight lines between the two circles, which divided the design into eight equal parts. Researchers held that this was a primitive version of the

换成了精致的玉签,简单的占卜变成了配以天地四方、太阳崇拜等复杂内涵的高级仪式。在贾湖—大汶口文化中,地位较高的人都可以拥有龟甲,或可以行使占卜之权,但到了凌家滩时期,龟甲则成了由极个别人使用的神秘工具,占卜行为甚至成了最高权威的体现。于是,原始的龟灵崇拜演化成了史前宗教文化,多数人可以随身携带的物品变成了由个别人掌管的部族圣物,原始占卜行为变成了决定部族命运和行使生杀大权的神秘仪式。古老的占卜术、原始的八卦文化在凌家滩文化中得到了升华并逐步走向成熟。

在距今 8000 年的淮河上游贾湖遗址出土的刻符龟甲(信阳学院冯春晓摄影)
Tortoise Shell with Engraved Symbols Unearthed in the Jiahu Site Dating Back to 8,000 Years Ago in the Upper Reaches of the Huaihe River(Photography by Feng Chunxiao, Xinyang University)

起源于淮河流域的这种古老的龟灵崇拜占卜方式直接开启了我国传统的八卦文化和易经文化,同时也启发了商人用钻灼牛骨、龟甲定吉凶的方法。

Chinese Eight Diagrams.

Artifacts unearthed in the Lingjiatan site reflect tendencies of the sun worship, bird worship and tortoise worship of ancestors in the Huaihe River Basin, with their main source being the Dawenkou Culture of Dongyi tribe. During the period of the Dawenkou Culture, a branch of Dongyi people migrated from Shandong Province to areas between the Yangtze River and the Huaihe River in Anhui Province, absorbing the local indigenous culture, and at the same time integrating the surrounding prehistoric culture, thus forming a new and unique culture. The Lingjiatan people further developed tortoise worship in the Jiahu-Dawenkou Culture: the materials used in tortoise worship ceremony have been changed from the original tortoise shells of natural creatures to those jade ones, homely artifacts such as stones and spicula placed within the tortoise shells have been replaced by delicate jade lots, and simple divination has evolved into a high-level ceremony with complex connotations such as the worship of four sides of heaven and earth and the sun. In Jiahu-Dawenkou Culture, all those with higher status could possess tortoise shells or exercise the power of divination, but in the Lingjiatan period, tortoise shells became mysterious tools used by very few selected people, and divination even became the embodiment of the highest authority. Thus, the primitive tortoise worship evolved into a prehistoric religious culture, items that most people had carried became tribal relics manipulated by the elites, and the primitive divination became a mysterious ceremony to determine the fate of the tribe and exercise the power of life and death. In this way, antique divination and primitive Eight Diagrams culture in the Lingjiatan Culture was sublimated and gradually matured.

Originating from the Huaihe River Basin, this antique divination method of tortoise worship directly opened up the traditional Eight Diagrams culture and I-Ching culture of China, and also inspired the merchants to use the methods of burnt ox bone and tortoise shell to predict good or bad luck.

三、淮河流域与汉字的发展

　　汉字的起源是一个十分复杂的问题，从有刻划符号到图形文字再到一定范围、一定时间连续使用的文字符号，然后到较为成熟的系统文字需要一个漫长的历史时期。从我们的先民开始使用某种图形或字符表达他们的思想的时候，文字的创作时代也就开始了。从这时起到商代的系统文字，中间需要数千年乃至上万年，或许更长一些时间。

　　关于旧石器时代的文字资料今天知之甚少，只有个别地方的早期岩画可以视为那一时期图形文字或文字的雏形。随着考古发现的不断深入，各种文物证据表明：至少从新石器时代早期开始，我们的祖先已经在其制作的陶器、石器等生活用品上通过刻划某些符号、绘制抽象的图案来传达某种思想或作为某种标识。尽管这些不能算是后来我们所认可的汉字，但却是汉字的雏形，是汉字在发展过程中必不可少的一环。从这个意义上来说，这些刻划符号与图形正是汉字的起源。

　　在淮河上游贾湖遗址出土的龟甲、石器、陶器上发现有一些刻划符号，初步统计共有十六例。按照今天的文字辨识标准或辨识习惯，这些符号很像"目""九""乙""甲""八""日""永"等，而且与后来商代殷墟出土的甲骨文中的写法十分相似。在淮河中游的安徽蚌埠双墩遗址发现了数量更多的刻划符号，这些符号大多数是刻划在陶碗的外圈足内，也有少数在外腹部和器物的圈足内。双墩器物上的刻划符号既有简单的汉字形状，也有具有象形意义的图画状，比如"十"字形、三角形、圆圈形、鹿形、鱼形、网状形、猪形、建筑物形、蚕形、花瓣形等。从众多的图案、符号来看，它是一套刻划讲究、应用范围较广、表意较为成熟的系统符号。在淮河下游大汶口文化圈中，也发现了一些文字符号，大汶口文化中的文字符号主要出现在陶尊或陶瓮上面，故而也称为陶尊文字。目前，此类陶尊文字或符号共发现二十四例，有"日""月"

III. The Huaihe River Basin and the Evolution of Chinese Characters

To trace the origin of Chinese characters is a very complicated issue. It took a long period for its evolution from carving symbols, graphic characters, literal symbols used uninterruptedly in a certain range and a certain period of time, and finally to a relatively mature character system. The age of writing came when our ancestors began to express their ideas with certain graphs or characters, and from then on until the formation of the systematic writing in the Shang Dynasty, it took thousands, even tens of thousands of years.

Evidence of characters in the Paleolithic period could scarcely be found today, and only a few early rock paintings could be regarded as graphic scripts or prototypes of writing in that period. With the deepening of archaeological discoveries, evidence from all kinds of cultural relics showed that our ancestors, at least starting from the early Neolithic Age, had begun to carve some symbols or drawn abstract designs on their hand-crafted daily necessities such as their pottery and stone artifacts to convey certain ideas or serve as certain kind of marking. These, though, not recognizable as the Chinese characters of today, could be seen as an embryonic form of Chinese characters and an essential link in the process of their evolution. In this sense, these carved symbols and figures were actually the origin of Chinese characters.

Some carved symbols, amounting to roughly 16 cases, were found on the unearthed tortoise shells, stone artifacts and pottery from the Jiahu site in the upper reaches of the Huaihe River. According to contemporary criterion and practice of character recognition, these symbols are most likely the Chinese characters 目 (eye), 九 (nine), 乙 (the 2nd of the Ten Heavenly Stems), 甲 (the 1st of the Ten Heavenly Stems), 八 (eight), 日 (sun) and 永 (lasting) etc., which are quite similar to those of inscriptions on oracle bones unearthed subsequently in the Yin Ruins of the Shang Dynasty. A larger number of carved symbols were found at the Shuangdun site in Bengbu, Anhui Province in the middle reaches of the Huaihe River. Most of these symbols were carved inside the outer ring feet of pottery bowls, and a few, on the outer belly or inside the ring feet of artifacts. The

"山""斤""斧""锛""炅""戌""旦""皇""凡""南""享"等。

安徽蚌埠双墩遗址发现的刻划符号（信阳学院冯春晓摄影）
Carved Symbols Found at the Shuangdun Site in Bengbu, Anhui Province(Photography by Feng Chunxiao, Xinyang University)

　　上述这些具有表意、记事功能的区域性文字符号或图案尽管不能称为成熟的汉字，更不可能是广为流传的系统文字，但却经过一个群体在同一时期的使用，并通过文化交流的方式得以在一定范围内传播，最终经过发展而成为后代汉字的有机组成部分。从这个意义上来说，淮河流域也是我国文字的一个重要的起源地。

carved symbols on the Shuangdun artifacts presented in the forms of both simple Chinese characters and pictographic ones, such as cross, triangle, circle, deer, fish, net, pig, building, silkworm and petal, etc. When taking these numerous graphics and symbols into consideration, it already displayed a set of systematic symbols, delicate carved, widely used and mature in expression. Some literal symbols largely appearing on the pottery statues and urns, were also found in the Dawenkou cultural circle in the lower reaches of the Huaihe River, so they were also called pottery statue characters. At present, examples of this kind of pottery character or symbol found amounted to 24, including those like 日 (sun), 月 (moon), 山 (mountain), 斤 (a unit of measurement which equals to 0.5 kilogram), 斧 (axe), 锛 (adze), 炅 (sunlight), 戌 (the eleventh of the Twelve Earthly Branches), 旦 (dawn), 皇 (emperor), 凡 (ordinary), 南 (south) and 享 (enjoy), etc.

These above-mentioned regional symbols or patterns with ideographic and memory functions, though, could neither be acknowledged as mature Chinese characters, nor be the widely spread systematic ones, eventually became the organic components of successive Chinese characters through the use of certain community in a certain period and the spread in a certain range through cultural communication. In this sense, the Huaihe River Basin is also an important cradle of the Chinese script.

四、淮河流域是我国稻作农业的重要起源地

从物质层面讲，一个区域稻作农业的发展代表着文明的一大进步，它是人类从游牧生活走向定居生活的重要标志。淮河流域最晚在新石器时代中期便已开始种植人工培育的水稻。淮河上游地区，在距今 8000 多年的贾湖遗址的一些红烧土块内发现了保存很好的稻壳印痕，经过鉴定，这些水稻属于人工栽培，而非野生。同时在贾湖遗址还出土了大量用来翻土的石铲，用于收割水稻等农作物的齿刃石镰，用来加工水稻等谷物的石磨盘、石磨棒等，这些都表明贾湖人不仅水稻种植达到了一个非常高的水平，而且对水稻的加工、利用也达到了很高水平。淮河中下游地区，在距今 8000 余年的顺山集遗址、距今 7000 多年的双墩遗址、距今 6000 多年的龙虬庄遗址和距今 5000 年的尉迟寺遗址等处，都出土有人工培育的水稻。

贾湖遗址出土的新石器时代的碳化稻谷（信阳学院冯葆炜拍摄整理）
Carbonized Unhusked Rice of the Neolithic Age Unearthed in Jiahu Site
(Photography by Feng Baowei, Xinyang University)

IV. The Huaihe River Basin—An Important Cradle of Chinese Paddy Agriculture

At the material level, the development of paddy agriculture in a region represents a great leap of civilization, and it is an important symbol of human beings' transition from nomadic life to settled life. The Huaihe River Basin as early as in the middle Neolithic Age, saw the manual planting of rice. In the upper reaches of the Huaihe River, well-preserved vestiges of rice husks were found in some burnt clay blocks at the Jiahu site dating back to more than 8,000 years ago, which was authenticated as manually planted rather than growing wild. In addition, a large number of stone shovels for soil aeration, toothed stone sickles for harvesting, and stone millstones and stone rods for grinding were found. All these indicated that the Jiahu people had achieved a high level of development not only in rice planting, but also in its processing and utilization. In the middle and lower reaches of the Huaihe River, manually planted rice has been unearthed in different sites such as the Shunshanji site dating back to 8,000 years ago, the Shuangdun site dating back to 7,000 years ago, as well as the Longqiuzhuang site dating back to 6,000 years ago, and the Yuchi Temple site dating back to 5,000 years ago.

Professor Zhang Juzhong held that the areas to the south of the Yellow River, including the Huaihe River Basin, the Yangtze River Basin and the Zhujiang River Basin, could be regarded as one integrated region of paddy agriculture, while the Yangtze River Basin and the Huaihe River Basin most likely stepped into the stage of primitive rice planting around the same time.

Due to climatic reasons, food crop species in the north and south of China in the palaeoid period were notably different. Rice was largely planted in the Yangtze River Basin in the south while millet crops were more common in north China, including the Loess Plateau. Located in the transitional zone between the north and the south and simultaneously the transitional zone that between the rice farming area in south China and the dry farming area in north China, the agricultural cropping in the Huaihe River Basin also bore the characteristics of mixed cropping of rice and dry crops. Seeds of rice, wild soybean and other plants

所以张居中教授认为，可以把黄河以南包括淮河、长江和珠江流域当作同一个稻作农业起源地，而淮河流域与长江流域很可能同步进入了稻作农业的原栽培阶段。

由于气候的原因，我国上古时期南北所种粮食作物种类大有不同，南方的长江流域主要种植水稻，而华北和黄土高原地区则主要种植中国粟和黍类的作物。由于淮河流域是南北气候的过渡带，同时也是中国南方稻作农业区与北方旱作农业区的过渡地带，所以其农业作物也体现出水稻和旱作物混作的特点。贾湖文化遗址中已有水稻和旱作物混作的农业模式。在贾湖遗址中发现有水稻、野大豆等植物的种子；在双墩遗址的红烧土残块中也发现了水稻稻壳印痕，同时还有小麦族植物，薏苡、燕麦等植物的淀粉粒；顺山集遗址出土有薏苡、水稻、小麦族等植物淀粉粒。这种水稻和旱作物混作的耕作方式一直持续至今。

were found in the Jiahu site. The vestiges of rice husks, as well as starch grain of triticeae plants, coix lachryma-jobi, oats, were also found in the burnt clay residues at the Shuangdun site, and similar ones like starch grains of coix lachryma-jobi, rice and triticeae plants were also unearthed in the Shunshanji site. The tillage methods of mixed cropping of rice and dry crops have been inherited and developed right up until present times.

五、淮河流域与中华民族的形成

　　在新石器时代，多支文化在淮河上游和中游地区交汇、融合、发展。随着炎帝、黄帝族的势力进入中原地区，仰韶文化也进入淮河上游地区，以太昊、少昊氏为部族首领的东夷人力量得到快速发展。东夷部族在北辛文化基础上发展起来的大汶口—龙山文化也随着东夷部族人群的迁徙和文化的交流等原因而渐次进入淮河中游和上游地区；长江流域的屈家岭文化通过豫西南进入淮河上游地区，在豫南广泛传播，并与外来的仰韶文化、大汶口文化、龙山文化并存。多种文化因素相互交流与融合，最终为独具特色的中原文化形成奠定了基础。

　　与此同时，在淮河下游地区，大汶口和良渚文化这两种邻近的文化又有着长期的交流与影响。从考古发现来看，大汶口文化在早期阶段就与环太湖地区的崧泽文化有了一定的交流，这种交流到了良渚时期则显得更为频繁和密切。良渚文化的一些元素为大汶口—龙山文化所吸纳，又通过文化交流与人员迁徙等因素进入中原地区，为中原文化吸收并积淀下来，从而对后天的夏商周文明产生了一定影响，如良渚玉器中的玉琮、玉璧、玉钺，陶器中的鼎、豆、壶三者的组合等，都为此后的商周礼制文化所继承，从而成为后天中国古代文明的一部分。

商代饕餮纹鼎（信阳学院冯春晓摄影）

The Taotie Design Tripod in the Shang Dynasty (Photography by Feng Chunxiao, Xinyang University)

V. The Huaihe River Basin and the Formation of Chinese Nation

In the Neolithic Age, several branches of culture converged, integrated and developed in the upper and middle reaches of the Huaihe River. Meanwhile, with the influence of tribes as those of Yan Emperor and Huang Emperor penetrating into the Central Plains, the Yangshao Culture also started to influence the upper reaches of the Huaihe River region. The impact of the Dongyi people with Taihao and Shaohao as their tribal leaders, developed rapidly. The Dawenkou-Longshan Culture, developed by the Dongyi tribe based on the Beixin Culture, gradually penetrated into the middle and upper reaches of the Huaihe River with the migration of the Dongyi tribal community and through the cultural exchange. The Qujialing Culture of the Yangtze River Basin entered the upper reaches of the Huaihe River through southwest Henan and spread widely in south Henan, coexisting with those alien cultures such as the Yangshao Culture, the Dawenkou Culture and the Longshan Culture, which finally laid the foundation of the formation of unique Central Plains Culture.

Simultaneously, the two neighboring cultures—the Dawenkou Culture and the Liangzhu Culture in the lower reaches of the Huaihe River, maintained long-term communication and mutual influence. According to archaeological discoveries, there was certain degree of communication between the Dawenkou Culture and the Songze Culture around the Taihu Lake in the early stages, while this communication became more frequent and intimate in the Liangzhu period. Some elements of the Liangzhu Culture were absorbed by the Dawenkou-Longshan Culture, and then entered the Central Plains through cultural exchange and migration, and were absorbed by the Central Plains Culture and then accumulated, which accordingly cast influences upon the civilization of succeeding Xia, Shang and Zhou dynasties. For example, the triple combination of jade and pottery wares, that of jade *cong*, jade disc and jade tomahawk and pottery tripod, pottery stemmed cup and pottery kettle, were all inherited by the later ritual culture of the Shang and Zhou dynasties, which consist of part of the subsequent Chinese ancient civilization.

商代息国息父辛鼎（信阳学院冯春晓摄影）
The Xifu Tripod in the Xi Vassal State, Shang Dynasty (Photography by Feng Chunxiao, Xinyang University)

正是通过淮河流域这一特殊的过渡与交汇地带的文化融合作用，我国新石器时代几乎主要的文化谱系如裴李岗—贾湖文化、仰韶文化—中原龙山文化、北辛—大汶口—山东龙山文化、马家浜—崧泽—良渚文化、屈家岭文化跨越长江与黄河得以完成交流与融合，从而奠定了后天中国上古文化大融合、大发展的坚实基础。

经历夏商至西周和春秋战国时代，随着楚人势力的北渐，淮河流域不仅是楚人与中原诸侯争夺的前沿，同时也是中原文化与楚文化交流、碰撞、融合的黄金地带。当吴越势力从长江流域向北发展之时，吴越文化、齐鲁文化、中原文化与楚文化都在淮河流域相汇聚，从而实现了几大最具特色区域文化的大交流与大融合。至战国中后期，随着周代众多诸侯国的相继灭亡、不同族群之间的融合，以中原族群为主体的华夏民族的概念越来越清晰，以中原文化为核心的华夏文化也越来越丰富。淮河流域的族群融合、文化交流史不仅是先秦时期我国族群演化与文化融合的有机组成部分，更是这一时期族群与文化融合最具代表性的特征。

Taking advantage of the function of cultural integration in the Huaihe River Basin as the transitional and converging zone, and across the Yangtze River and the Huanghe River, almost all those main cultural genealogies in the Neolithic Age, including the Peiligang-Jiahu Culture, the Yangshao Culture, the Longshan Culture of the Central Plains, the Beixin-Dawenkou-Shandong Longshan Culture, the Majiabang-Songze-Liangzhu Culture and the Qujialing Culture, have been converged and integrated with each other, laying the solid foundation for the great integration of subsequent Chinese palaeoid cultures.

出土于信阳长台关 9 号墓的战国时期编钟（信阳学院冯春晓摄影）
Chime Bells of the Warring States Period Unearthed in the Changtaiguan No. 9 Tomb, Xinyang (Photography by Feng Chunxiao, Xinyang University)

Undergone the years from the Xia and Shang dynasties to the Western Zhou Dynasty and the Spring and Autumn and Warring States periods, the Huaihe River Basin became not only the frontier of the competition between the Chu people and the vassals of the Central Plains, but also the central zone of the communication, collision and integration of the Central Plains Culture and the Chu Culture. When the power of Wu and Yue kingdoms started their northward expansion from the Yangtze River Basin, cultures such as the Wu-Yue Culture,

河南息县发掘的距今 3500 年的淮河古沉船（信阳学院冯春晓摄影）
An Antique Shipwreck of the Huaihe River 3,500 Years Ago Excavated in Xixian County, Henan Province (Photography by Feng Chunxiao, Xinyang University)

the Qi-Lu Culture, the Central Plains Culture and the Chu Culture all converged here in the Huaihe River Basin, thus contributing to the great exchange and integration of those several most distinctive major regional cultures. In the middle and late Warring States Period, with the collapse of numerous vassal states in the Zhou Dynasty and the integration of different ethnic groups, the concept of the Chinese nation with the Central Plains ethnic group as the main body became more and more apparent, and the Chinese culture with the Central Plains Culture as the core became richer in connotation. The history of ethnic integration and cultural exchange in the Huaihe River Basin was not only an integral part of ethnic evolution and cultural integration in China during the pre-Qin period, but also the most representative feature of ethnic and cultural integration in this period.

第二章

根亲篇：淮河流域的移民与根亲文化

Chapter 2

Root Seeking: The Emigrant and Root Seeking

Culture in the Huaihe River Basin

在中国历史的长河中,淮河儿女,正如奔腾不息的千里淮河一样,不仅在祖先世代耕种的土地上繁衍生息,而且受各种因素影响不断向外迁徙。他们心怀桑梓,勇于奋进,谱写了一曲曲英雄的移民赞歌。伴随着移民播迁及移民与祖根地的持续交往,淮河流域的根亲文化日益深厚。根亲文化蕴含的精神是游子对故乡故土的深情眷恋,表达出的家国情怀则是镌刻在每一位淮河儿女心中不可磨灭的文化基因。

一、光州固始向福建的移民

在中国移民史上,光州固始(今信阳市固始县)大名鼎鼎。她与山西洪洞大槐树、湖北麻城孝感、广东珠玑巷、苏州阊门等地齐名,是我国著名的十大移民集散地之一。固始移民的主要方向是以福建为主的东南地区,又自福建持续向台湾及海外东南亚地区播迁。近年来,豫闽台三地普遍认同:台湾同胞的祖根500年前在福建,1300多年前在河南。台湾同胞来大陆寻根认亲,往往首站福建,终站河南固始,即"台湾访祖到福建,漳江思源溯固始"。固始是闽台以及东南亚很多姓氏的祖根地。

信阳师范学院尹全海教授等著的固始移民文化专著(信阳学院冯春晓摄影)
Monograph on Gushi Emigration Culture by Professor Yin Quanhai etc., Xinyang Normal University (Photography by Feng Chunxiao, Xinyang University)

In the long history of China, sons and daughters of the Huaihe River, just like her ever-flowing currents, not only lived and multiplied on the land cultivated by their ancestors for generations, but also emigrated uninterruptedly under the influence of various factors. They held their nostalgic sentiment to hometown, strived to forge ahead and succeeded in composing their heroic emigration anthems. With uninterrupted emigration and the close contact between emigrants and their ancestral land, the root seeking culture in the Huaihe River Basin was solidly established. The root seeking culture is bestowed with the spirit of affectionate homesickness to the hometown and homeland, while the profound love of the family and the nation has become the indelible cultural genes engraved in the hearts of every Huaihe River descendant.

I. The Emigration from Gushi Guangzhou to Fujian Province

In the history of Chinese migration, Gushi, Guangzhou (present Gushi County, Xinyang), together with Dahuaishu Village, Hongtong County in Shanxi Province, Xiaogan, Macheng City in Hubei Province, Zhuji Ancient Alley in Guangdong Province and Changmen in Suzhou City, is well known as one of the ten distributing centers of migration. The destination of Gushi emigrants is mainly the area in the southeast China, largely in Fujian Province, and then to areas as Taiwan and Southeast Asia. In recent years, it has been widely acknowledged, in Henan Province and Fujian Province as well as Taiwan, that the ancestral roots of Taiwan compatriots originated in Fujian 500 years ago and Henan 1,300 years ago. The first destination of Taiwanese to seek their roots in Chinese mainland is usually Fujian Province, and Gushi, the terminal destination, which is what we customarily describe "Fujian is the ancestral home of our Taiwan compatriots, while Gushi, the ancestral home of inhabitants along the Zhangjiang River in Fujian Province". And Gushi is the ancestral land contributing to the spreading of those numerous family names in Fujian, Taiwan and Southeast Asia.

Located in the east of Xinyang City, Gushi County, bearing the name that implies "solidity and initiation", has a history of nearly 2,000 years. It underwent

固始县位于信阳市东部，其得名取"坚固初始"之意，建县已有近2000年的历史。从汉代至宋有过四次固始向福建移民的浪潮，分别是汉末魏晋南北朝时期、唐代前期、唐代末期和两宋时期。

东汉末年，中原发生战乱，人民流离失所，四处逃亡，其中有很多迁至福建。如北宋榜眼黄宗旦追述自己的家史时称，他的祖先黄道隆就是东汉时期光州固始人，在建安之乱时弃官避地入闽。

西晋末永嘉年间，北方人又一次大批南迁。据《晋书·王导传》等史书记载，当时有百分之六七十的中州士女都南下避乱。其中林、陈、黄、郑、詹、邱、何、胡等八姓族人迁往福建居多，史称"八姓入闽"。

固始人移民至福建的第二个高潮期是唐朝前期。唐总章二年(669年)，泉州、潮州一带发生动乱，唐朝廷命令岭南行军总管固始人陈政率府兵将士3600名入闽平乱。第二年，陈政之兄陈敏、陈敷带领五十八姓军校南下支援，途中，陈敏、陈敷不幸相继病逝，陈母和陈政之子陈元光继续领兵前行，他们与陈政所领之军会合后平定了动乱。随

漳州威惠庙"开漳圣王"陈元光雕像（信阳学院冯春晓摄影）
Statue of Chen Yuanguang, the Sacred Pioneer of Zhangzhou, in Weihui Temple, Zhangzhou (Photography by Feng Chunxiao, Xinyang University)

four surges of Gushi to Fujian emigration from the Han to the Song Dynasty, respectively in the period of late Han, Wei and Jin, and Southern and Northern dynasties; in the early Tang Dynasty period; in the late Tang Dynasty period and the Northern and Southern Song dynasties.

At the end of the Eastern Han Dynasty, war broke out in the Central Plains. People were forced to leave their hometown and their perpetual settlements, and most of them emigrated to Fujian Province. When tracing his family history, Huang Zongdan, the 2nd place winner at the Palace Exam in the Northern Song Dynasty (960-1127 AD), claimed that his forefather Huang Daolong was a native of Gushi in Guangzhou (present Huangchuan County, Xinyang) during the Eastern Han Dynasty (25-220 AD), who abandoned his official position and fled to Fujian during the period of Jian'an Rebellion.

In the late Western Jin Dynasty during the reign of Yongjia Emperor, a large number of northerners emigrated southward. According to the records in the historical documents such as *Biography of Wang Dao in Book of Jin*, about 60 to 70 percent of the young men and women in the Central Region at that time went southward to escape the chaos. And among them, the clansmen of the eight families largely emigrated to Fujian Province, including those of Lin, Chen, Huang, Zheng, Zhan, Qiu, He and Hu family, historically known as "Emigration of Eight Families with Different Surnames to Min (Fujian Province)".

The early Tang Dynasty period witnessed the 2nd surge of Gushi emigration to Fujian Province. In the 2nd year (669 AD) of Zongzhang Eemperor of the Tang Dynasty, riots broke out around the Quanzhou and Chaozhou areas, Fujian Province. Together with his 3,600 family soldiers, Chen Zheng from Gushi, the military general of the Tang Dynasty, was sent by the court to launch a counter insurgency campaign in Fujian. In the following year, his two elder brothers—Chen Min and Chen Fu, together with some other soldiers from 58 clans, were also sent southward as the reinforcements. After the death of both the elder brothers in succession, their mother and Chen Yuanguang, the son of Chen Zheng, kept marching forward and succeeded in fulfilling the counter-insurgency mission with the combined efforts of the two military forces. Consequently, Zhangzhou Government was set by the royal court with Chen Yuanguang as the first governor. He took measures such as recruiting and placating those

后，朝廷新置漳州，陈元光被任命为首任漳州刺史，他招抚流亡，注重农业生产，兴办学校，劝民向化，鼓励军校府兵与当地土著居民通婚，缓解了移民与土著间的矛盾，促进了漳州经济文化的发展。陈元光逝世后，陈元光之子陈珦、孙陈酆、曾孙陈谟相继担任漳州刺史，他们祖孙几代人相继治漳，都颇有政绩。来自光州固始的移民与当地人一起筚路蓝缕开发漳州，使漳州从曾经的"蛮荒之地"变成了礼仪与富庶之地。人们感念陈元光的功绩，建祠纪念他，尊奉他为"开漳圣王"。后来随着移民及文化传播，"开漳圣王"信仰逐渐流传开来，成为闽台及东南亚地区的重要民间信仰。

唐朝末期，固始人第三次大批移民入闽。唐光启元年（885年），王审知、王潮、王审邦兄弟率兵5000人自光、寿两州南下，进入闽南，先居泉州，后尽有全闽之地。据考证，追随王审知兄弟入闽的固始籍移民有40多个姓氏，数量在二三万人。王审知占领福建后，采取了一系列促进福建发展的措施。经过治理，福建成为当时全国最为稳定繁荣的地方之一。因治闽功绩显著，王审知被尊称为"闽王""入闽人祖"。

入闽人祖王审知（信阳师范学院辛文迪绘画）
Wang Shenzhi—The Ancestor of Fujian Immigrants (Painting by Xin Wendi, Xinyang Normal University)

exiles, attaching importance to agriculture, setting up schools and eradicating barbarism. He also advocated miscegenation between the soldiers and the aboriginals, alleviating tensions between the immigrants and the locals and strong developments both economically and culturally were achieved in Zhangzhou. After the death of Chen Yuanguang, Chen Xiang, the son of Chen Yuanguang, together with Chen Feng the grandson and Chen Mo the great-grandson, was appointed to be successive governor of Zhangzhou, all winning prestige for their political achievements. Immigrants from Gushi, Guangzhou, together with the aboriginals, blazed the trail for the development of Zhangzhou and contributed to turning Zhangzhou from the barbarian land to a richly endowed county. To commemorate Chen Yuanguang, a temple was built for him and he was honored as the "Sacred Pioneer of Zhangzhou", and the "Sacred Pioneer" worship, with the consistent emigration and the cultural transmission, gradually spread out and became the dominant non-governmental belief in the region of Fujian, Taiwan and Southeast Asia.

At the end of the Tang Dynasty, Gushi people started their 3rd large-scale emigration to Fujian Province. In the first year of Guangqi Emperor's reign (885 AD), Wang Shenzhi, Wang Chao and Wang Shengui brothers commanded 5,000 soldiers from Guangzhou and Shouzhou down south into southern Fujian. They first of all stationed at Quanzhou and then expanded their influence all over Fujian. Studies have showed that those Gushi immigrants following Wang Shenzhi brothers to Fujian amounted to 20 to 30 thousand, involving more than 40 different surnames. A series of measures to facilitate the development of Fujian were taken by Wang Shenzhi when taking control of the province. Under his governance, Fujian became one of the most stable and prosperous areas in the nation, and Wang Shenzhi, then, was venerated as "King of Fujian" and "the Ancestor of Fujian Immigrants" for his striking achievements in the governance of Fujian.

During the Southern and Northern Song dynasties, with the southward shift of the economic center, the migrants started uninterruptedly their southward migration from the Central Plains to places like Fujian. After the Jingkang Riots, Zhao Gou proclaimed himself emperor (i.e. Emperor Gaozong in the Song Dynasty) at Nanjing (present Shangqiu, Henan Province), historically known

两宋时期，经济重心南移，不断有移民自中原南迁至福建等地。"靖康之变"后赵构在南京（今河南商丘）称帝（即宋高宗），史称南宋。后南宋政府南迁扬州，再迁至镇江，又迁至杭州。很多中原人跟随朝廷南迁，再次掀起了向东南或长江以南移民的高潮。

自汉至宋数百年间，固始人四次大规模播迁至福建，入籍定居，繁衍生息，为东南沿海边陲带去了百余姓氏。这些移民与当地人民通婚繁衍，其后裔逐渐构成了福建民众的主体，为日后福建人继续向台湾与海外播迁奠定了基础。

as the Southern Song Dynasty. Later the court relocated first of all the capital southward to Yangzhou, then to Zhenjiang and Hangzhou. Many inhabitants in the Central Plains then migrated southward with the royal court, which started once again an upsurge of southeastward migration and migration to the south of the Yangtze River.

For centuries from the Han Dynasty to the Song Dynasty, Gushi people settled down and thrived in Fujian. The four surges of large-scale southward migration brought to the southeast coastal frontiers hundreds of surnames. These immigrants intermarried with the local people and their descendants gradually made up the majority of Fujian inhabitants, which paved the way for the subsequent migration of Fujian inhabitants to Taiwan and overseas.

二、固始移民由福建向台湾和海外的播迁

1. 福建移民向台湾迁徙

元明清时期，随着经济发展和人口繁衍，福建逐渐由人少地多变成了人多地少，人地矛盾逐渐突出。福建开始大量向外输出人口，台湾是当时福建人口迁移的主要方向。

明天启元年（1621年），海澄（今漳州市龙海区）人颜思齐在台湾筑寨以居，镇抚土番。颜思齐死后，郑芝龙接替颜思齐继续经营台湾，他在福建布政使熊文灿的支持下，招募沿海数万灾民，每人给三两银子，每三人给一头牛，用大船装载，将他们运到台湾去垦殖。荷兰人窃踞台湾后，也曾在闽南沿海招募移民去台湾开荒拓土。清朝顺治十八年（1661年），郑成功赶走荷兰人，收复了台湾。他所带领的士兵连同眷属共3万余人都留在台湾开荒种植。郑成功还到漳州、泉州、兴化等地招募青壮年到台湾垦荒。陈孔立教授在《清代台湾移民社会研究》一书中提出，根据台湾耕地面积进行估算，郑氏时代台湾的汉人人口在10万～12万人。1683年之后，台湾受清政府管辖，福建等东南地区继续向台湾多次移民。

连横在其所著《台湾通史》中说："台湾之人，中国之人也，而又闽粤之族也。"这句话强调了台湾与大陆闽粤地区的血脉联系。据台湾地区各姓家谱记载，其先祖大多来自光州固始，是跟随唐初陈元光父子或唐末王审知兄弟入闽，后又在明清时期逐渐迁入台湾。台湾各姓中，陈、林、黄、郑人口最多。台湾谚语中有"陈林半天下，黄郑排满街"的说法。

陈姓源自河南，在台湾支派众多，开漳圣王派是其最重要的支派之一。从地区来说，台湾陈姓主要有三种情况：一是来自福建的泉州、同安；二是来自漳州下辖的漳浦、南靖、平和等县；三是来自广东的蕉岭、长乐、平远等地。

II. Migration of Gushi Migrants from Fujian to Taiwan and Overseas

1. The Migration from Fujian to Taiwan

In the Yuan, Ming and Qing dynasties, Fujian underwent a transition from the situation of a small population with rich land resources to a large population with a deficiency of land due to the economic development and population growth. The contradiction between population and land was gradually and strikingly highlighted. Large-scale population emigration started then in Fujian and the major destination was Taiwan.

In the first year of Tianqi Emperor's reign (1621 AD), Ming Dynasty, Yan Siqi, a Haicheng (present Longhai District, Zhangzhou City) inhabitant started to build settlements in Taiwan, and pacified those seigniors. After his death, Zheng Zhilong succeeded him and continued to run Taiwan. Backed by Xiong Wencan, the administrative commissioner of Fujian Province, he recruited tens of thousands of victims of natural calamities along the coastal areas and shipped them to Taiwan to reclaim and plant, redistributing resources, including 3 *liang* (150 grams) silver ingot per person, and a head of cattle per 3 people. At the time the Dutch had colonized Taiwan, they also recruited immigrants from the coastal areas of southern Fujian to open up land in Taiwan. In the 18th year of Shunzhi Emperor's reign, Qing Dynasty (1661 AD), Zheng Chenggong succeeded in sending Dutch packing and took Taiwan under his administration. Soldiers under his commanding together with their family members, amounting to 30 thousand, then resided there, reclaiming and planting. He also recruited youngsters in their prime around Zhangzhou, Quanzhou and Xinghua for the same purpose. In his academic monograph *A Study on the Immigrant Society of Taiwan in the Qing Dynasty*, professor Chen Kongli holds that the population of ethnic Han under Zheng Chenggong's administration is estimated to be 100 thousand to 120 thousand when taking the farmland acreage into consideration. After 1683, Taiwan came under the jurisdiction of the Qing Government, and emigration in southeast regions including Fujian to Taiwan continued apace.

In his monograph *General History of Taiwan*, Lian Heng insists that

林姓也源自河南，卫辉是林姓发源地。中原人屡次南迁，都有众多的林姓人。如唐初随陈政、陈元光入闽的林行实，在福建以及台湾都有重要的历史影响。《溪环社林氏族谱》记载，林行实是今漳州市浦南镇溪园村林氏始祖，原籍河南光州固始，是陈政的九女婿，唐高宗时随陈氏父子入闽，后代在福建及台湾播迁者甚众。此外，唐末随王审知入闽的林姓人有林延皓、林延甲、林穆等，他们分别被尊称为"控鹤林氏""后安林氏""陶江林氏"的入闽始祖。明清时期，林姓人也大量渡台。

台湾黄姓是仅次于陈姓和林姓的人口大姓。黄姓的重要发源地是先

郑成功雕像
The Statue of Zheng Chenggong

Taiwanese are descendants of people of Fujian and Guangdong provinces. The statement highlighted the blood ties between Taiwan and regions of Fujian and Guangdong in Chinese mainland. According to the genealogical records of various family names in Taiwan, most of their ancestors came from Gushi, Guangzhou. They followed Chen Yuanguang and his son in the early Tang Dynasty or Wang Shenzhi and his brothers in the late Tang Dynasty to Fujian, and then gradually emigrated to Taiwan in the Ming and Qing dynasties. In Taiwan, the most common family names are Chen, Lin, Huang and Zheng. There is a saying in Taiwan, "Those with the family name of Chen or Lin take a half of the population, while those of Huang or Zheng may block the streets."

The family name of Chen is originated from Henan Province with multitudinous branches in Taiwan, while the Sacred Pioneer of Zhangzhou school being one of the most important. In terms of regions, the family name of Chen in Taiwan presents largely in the following three cases: one is from Quanzhou and Tong'an in Fujian Province, the second is from counties like Zhangpu, Nanjing and Pinghe under the jurisdiction of Zhangzhou, and the third is from regions like Jiaoling, Changle and Pingyuan in Guangdong Province.

The family name of Lin is also originated from Henan Province with Weihui County as her source. Many people with the family name of Lin are descended from the southward migrations of the Central Plains inhabitants. E.g., Lin Xingshi, the follower of Chen Zheng and Chen Yuanguang's Fujian emigration, cast significant historical influence on both Fujian Province and Taiwan. According to *The Lin Family Genealogy of Xihuan Society*, Lin Xingshi was the first ancestor of the Lin family in Xiyuan Village, Punan Town, Zhangzhou City. With Gushi, Guangzhou in Henan Province as his ancestral home, Lin Xingshi, the ninth son-in-law of Chen Zheng, following his father-in-law and uncle to Fujian during Emperor Gaozong's reign in the Tang Dynasty, and many descendants of him migrated to Fujian and Taiwan. In addition, the family members of Lin that migrated to Fujian by following Wang Shenzhi at the end of the Tang Dynasty were Lin Yanhao, Lin Yanjia and Lin Mu, who were esteemed respectively as the earliest Fujian immigration ancestor of "Konghe Lin", "Hou'an Lin" and "Taojiang Lin". During the Ming and Qing dynasties, family members of Lin also migrated to Taiwan in large numbers.

秦时期的黄国，黄国即在信阳潢川县，毗邻固始。黄国被楚灭后，国人以国为姓，四处播迁。从固始入闽的四次移民大浪潮中，黄姓都是重要的移民姓氏。黄姓渡台也很早。宋末元初，福建黄氏为了逃避元兵捕杀，开始举家渡海入台。在明、清两代，黄氏是迁台的主力军之一。

台湾郑姓中影响最大的莫过于收复台湾的民族英雄福建南安郑成功家族。据《郑成功族谱三种》中郑芝鸾（郑成功族叔）序云：其祖随王潮自光州固始入闽，后传至郑绍祖，生子五人，依次是郑芝龙、郑芝虎、郑芝鹏、郑芝鸾、郑芝豹。郑芝龙即郑成功之父，他早年流亡日本，后乘明末动乱之机在东南沿海发展，成为海上最大的民间力量，经明朝招抚后归顺明朝廷。明清鼎革之际，郑成功从荷兰人手中收复了台湾，以台湾为根据地对抗清朝。康熙二十二年（1683年），清政府派施琅招降

厦门郑成功纪念馆
Zheng Chenggong Memorial Hall in Xiamen

The family name of Huang is the 3rd largest population in Taiwan only after that of Chen and Lin. The family name of Huang is originated from the Huang Kingdom in the pre-Qin period, i.e., present Huangchuan County, Xinyang City, which is next to Gushi County. After being overthrown by the Chu Kingdom, people of Huang took the title of the kingdom as their family name and migrated in all directions. The family name of Huang contributed a lot as an important migration family name in the four migration upsurges from Gushi to Fujian. Family members of Huang also emigrated to Taiwan as early as in the late Song and early Yuan dynasties. To avoid being captured and killed by Yuan soldiers, many migrated across the Strait to Taiwan. And up to the Ming and Qing dynasties, people with the family name of Huang were still the majority among migrants to Taiwan.

The family of Zheng Chenggong in Nan'an, Fujian is without question the most influential among the family name of Zheng in Taiwan due to his recapturing Taiwan from the hands of the Dutch and since then he himself was honored as national hero. According to the prologue of *Zheng Chenggong Family Genealogy of Three Kinds* by Zheng Zhiluan (uncle of Zheng Chenggong), following Wang Chao, the family ancestor emigrated from Gushi, Guangzhou to Fujian, and up to the generation of Zheng Shaozu, the family gave birth to five sons, namely Zheng Zhilong, Zheng Zhihu, Zheng Zhipeng, Zheng Zhiluan and Zheng Zhibao. Zheng Zhilong, the father of Zheng Chenggong, exiled to Japan in his early years, and then taking the advantage of unrest during the late Ming Dynasty, returned to the southeast coastal areas to make a living, going on to control one of the strongest private fleets on the sea, then converting to serve the royal court of the Ming Dynasty after having been promised amnesty. At the turning point of the Ming and Qing dynasties, Zheng Chenggong recaptured Taiwan from the hands of the Dutch and made it a base to resist the Qing Dynasty. In the 22nd year of Emperor Kangxi's reign (1683 AD), Shi Lang, appointed by the Qing Government, summoned him to surrender, which terminated his domination of Taiwan and Taiwan was finally back in the domain of the Qing Dynasty.

In short, since the Yuan, Ming and Qing dynasties, many immigrants with different surnames represented by Chen, Lin, Huang and Zheng from Fujian and

了郑氏,将台湾收归版图,郑氏对台湾的统治宣告结束。

总之,元明清以来,以陈、林、黄、郑等姓氏为代表,诸多来自福建等地的各姓移民不惧台湾海峡的惊涛骇浪,毅然渡海迁台,他们定居台湾后,披荆斩棘,凿井辟田,为开发和建设台湾做出了突出贡献。

2. 福建移民向海外播迁

明清时期,福建等沿海地区也掀起了向东南亚地区移民的高潮,史称"下南洋"。移民自福建漳州、泉州、福州等地出发,通过香港、澳门、厦门、汕头等口岸出境,乘船南行,历尽艰难曲折,到达新加坡、马来西亚、泰国、印度尼西亚、菲律宾等国家谋求发展。在这些旅居海外的华人中,时时会涌现出来一些杰出人物,他们不仅在当地很有声望,为社会发展做出了突出贡献,而且始终心系祖国和故土,时时刻刻不忘桑梓,也为祖国发展贡献了许多力量。

著名爱国华侨领袖陈嘉庚先生,原籍福建,17岁时前往新加坡,先是跟随父亲经营米店,后成为华侨中最大橡胶垦殖者之一,被称为新加坡、马来西亚橡胶王国的四大开拓者之一。他开办有橡胶制品厂、米厂、皮鞋厂等产业,积极兴办教育,在促进当地经济发展的同时,也积极支持祖国反抗日本侵略者斗争和新中国建设事业。

林姓华人在东南亚地区的影响也非常大,历史上涌现出了许多实业巨子、爱国志士。如印尼前首富林绍良先生祖籍福州福清县,20多岁时移民印尼,经过多年苦心经营,构建起了自己的林氏王国,经营范围涉及多个行业,产业分布在印尼、新加坡、荷兰、美国及中国香港等国家和地区,他也积极在中国大陆投资,涉及房地产、金融和酒店等领域。

黄姓也是东南亚地区人数较多的大姓,他们移民至海外后,遵守当地法律,与当地人民友好相处,创基立业,披荆斩棘,艰苦拼搏,培育出大批先贤时杰。如在菲律宾的华侨中,黄姓人数仅次于陈姓。

other places, braving the stormy waves of the Taiwan Strait, resolutely migrated to Taiwan. After settling in Taiwan, they carved a path through brambles and thorns, and made outstanding contributions to the development and construction of Taiwan.

2. Overseas Migration of Fujian Migrants

In the Ming and Qing dynasties, an upsurge of migration to Southeast Asia started from southeast coastal areas including Fujian, historically known as "Voyage Down to Southeast Asia". Migrants from Zhangzhou, Quanzhou and Fuzhou departed from ports like Hong Kong, Macau, Xiamen and Shantou, and boarded the southbound ships. They underwent arduous and tortuous journeys, and finally arrived at Singapore, Malaysia, Thailand, Indonesia and Philippines. Among those overseas Chinese, some joined the elites but although they became prestigious in these societies, contributing a lot to the social development, they always held a nostalgic sentiment for their hometown and native country and strove for the development of their homeland.

Mr. Tan Kah Kee, the famous patriotic overseas Chinese leader, was a Fujianese who emigrated to Singapore at the age of 17. He started his business as a manager of the rice shop together with his father, and later became one of the largest rubber growers among overseas Chinese, known as one of the four pioneers of the rubber kingdom of Singapore and Malaysia. He set up a rubber products factory, a rice factory, a leather shoe factory and other industries and actively participated in the nourishment of education while helping to promote the local economic development. He also made notable efforts to support the Anti-Japanese War in homeland and the construction cause of the People's Republic of China.

Overseas Chinese with the family name of Lin also cast great influence on Southeast Asia. There emerged large numbers of industrial tycoons and patriots among them. As an example, Mr. Lin Shaoliang, formerly richest man in Indonesia, emigrated from Fuqing County in his 20s and established his own business empire after years of painstaking efforts. His business covered various industries and different countries and regions, including Indonesia, Singapore, the Netherlands, the United States, and Hong Kong of China. He also actively

总而言之,"下南洋"是明清以来中国历史上最为重大的移民活动之一。这些移民及其后裔播迁海外,成为旅居世界各地的华人华侨,他们在异国他乡艰苦创业,造福当地也传播华夏文化,为世界文明进步做出了宝贵贡献,赢得了国际社会的广泛赞誉。

participated in investment in Chinese mainland, covering the fields of real estate, finance and hotels, etc.

The family name of Huang is also strongly represented in Southeast Asia's population. After their emigration overseas, they abode by local laws, and got along well with the locals. They laid foundations for their careers and strove for success by overcoming all difficulties, and were well represented at all levels of society. For example, among the overseas Chinese in the Philippines, the population with Huang as surname is the 2nd only to that of Chen.

In conclusion, "Voyage Down to Southeast Asia" was one of the most important migration campaigns in Chinese history since the Ming and Qing dynasties. These emmigrants, together with their descendants, emigrated overseas and settled in different parts of the world. They worked hard in foreign lands, benefited local people, and spread Chinese culture as well so as to make valuable contributions to the progress of the world civilization, winning unanimous praise from the international community.

三、姓氏寻根到中原

"树高千尺不忘根",中华炎黄子孙对祖源地都有着天然的、深深的眷恋之情,这就是"根亲"意识。因此,中华儿女不管播迁至何地,都不忘追寻自身的血缘和血脉。1981年黄典诚教授在《河南日报》上发表《寻根母语到中原》一文,提出台湾同胞的寻根起点是闽南,而终点则为河南,由此拉开了闽台及海外各姓宗亲到河南固始寻根探亲的序幕。

1. 改革开放至20世纪末的根亲活动

20世纪最后20年,台湾民众自发寻根的愿望日益强烈,他们的行动引起了社会各界的广泛关注,成为一个社会热点问题。学术界也围绕移民及根亲文化进行了大量建设性的学术研究。

1978年,台湾报纸《青年战士报》上连续刊文,介绍台湾与大陆姓氏、宗族、文化、风俗等方面的联系,指出台湾的祖根在大陆。同年,台湾"中央图书馆"举办了"根——台湾的过去和未来"的文物图片展,用多件文物资料实证台湾的祖根是大陆。之后,台湾各界广泛讨论台湾的祖根问题,确认了台湾与大陆之间的血脉亲情,其祖根是福建等地。

与此同时,大陆也开始进行姓氏文化及根亲文化研究。1982年,河南信阳地委组织召开了台湾同胞祖根问题座谈会,信阳师范学院成立了台湾同胞祖根问题研究会。1980年著名学者欧潭生先生撰写《一千年前是一家——台闽豫祖根渊源初探》一文,后又撰写《台闽豫祖根渊源再探——兼论何处是郑成功之墓》一文,从台湾历史和姓氏谱牒入手,探讨台湾与福建、固始之间的祖根渊源问题。1989年,顺应海外返乡寻根的热潮,福建姓氏源流研究会成立,成为开展豫闽台姓氏文化源流研究的重要机构。

III. Central Plains Ancestral Root Seeking of Different Families

As a Chinese saying goes, "Trees towering thousands of feet are nurtured by their roots." The descendants of Chinese nation hold profound affection to their ancestral home, which is what we call the conscience of ancestral root seeking. In his article "Seeking Roots of Mother Tongue to the Central Plains" published in *Henan Daily* in 1981, Professor Huang Diancheng proposed that the starting point of Taiwanese searching for their roots is in south Fujian, and the terminus is Henan, which opened the prelude of root seeking of overseas Chinese with various family names to Gushi, Henan Province.

1. Root-seeking Activities from the Reform and Opening-up to the End of the 20th Century

In the last two decades of the 20th century, the aspiration of the spontaneous root seeking was increasingly intensified among Taiwan compatriots. It caught widespread attention from all levels of the society and became a hot issue, with large quantities of academic researches focusing on immigration and root-seeking culture being carried out in academic circles.

A series of articles were published in the newspaper *The Youth Warrior* in Taiwan in 1978, which introduced the relationship between Chinese mainland and Taiwan through family names, clans, culture and customs, highlighting the fact that the ancestral root of Taiwan is in Chinese mainland. Held in the same year, a photo exhibition of cultural relics, Root—Taiwan: Past and Future, further confirmed this. After this, there arose the extensive discussion on the issue of roots of Taiwan and a common agreement reached that there existed deep ties between Chinese mainland and Taiwan, and that the roots of Taiwan were in places like Fujian Province.

Similarly in Chinese mainland, researches on family name and root-seeking culture also started. In 1982, a conference was held on the roots of Taiwan compatriots by CPC Xinyang Prefecture, Henan, and Taiwan Compatriots Ancestral Root Issue Research Association was also founded in Xinyang Normal

固始根亲文化节（夏义摄影）
Gushi Root-seeking Culture Festival (Photography by Xia Yi)

1987年，台湾开放大陆探亲，台湾人纷纷申请返乡探亲祭祖，很多人回到闽南漳泉祖籍地以及河南寻根谒祖，这成为当时豫闽台民间交往的热点。除了台湾，海外宗亲也纷纷组团赴河南寻根。20世纪90年代的十年间，至少有37批次宗亲来河南寻根，包括叶、郑、赖、林、钟、黄、陈、蔡等姓，其中赴信阳寻亲的主要有：1995年4月，菲律宾江夏黄氏宗亲会34人赴信阳潢川祭祖寻根；1996年4月，新加坡南洋黄氏联谊会寻根恳亲代表团33人赴信阳潢川祭祖寻根；1996年5月，息县赖氏文化研究会邀请海内外宗亲举行"纪念叔颖公受封立国3118周年大会"；1997年4月，马来西亚、新加坡以及中国港澳台地区赖氏宗亲会96人参加"纪念赖氏始祖叔颖公受封立国3119周年暨赖罗付谒祖大典"等。

University in the same year. Ou Tansheng, a famous scholar, wrote two theses, i.e.: "On the Ancestral Roots of Taiwan, Fujian and Henan—One Family a Thousand Years Ago" and "Further Research on the Ancestral Roots of Taiwan, Fujian and Henan—and A Query on Tomb of Zheng Chenggong" respectively in 1980 and after, in which he discussed the issue on the relationship among Fujian, Gushi and Taiwan through ancestral roots from the perspective of Taiwan's history and genealogy of family names. To cater to the homeward root-seeking upsurge of overseas compatriots, Seminar on Filiation of Fujian Family Names was founded in 1981 and became the institution for the study of filiation of family name culture in Henan, Fujian and Taiwan.

In 1987, Taiwan compatriots were allowed to visit the mainland and they began to apply for their homeward journey to visit kinsmen and offer sacrifices to their ancestors. Among them, many were back to their ancestral homeland in Zhangzhou and Quanzhou in south Fujian Province and also Henan Province, which became the hot issue of the civil communication among Henan, Fujian and Taiwan. Meanwhile, compatriots overseas also went back to Henan for their root-seeking journey. In the last decade of 1990s, there were at least 37 groups of clansmen who visited Henan for their root-seeking journey, including family members of different family names, such as Ye, Zheng, Lai, Lin, Zhong, Huang, Chen and Cai, etc. Among those who visited Xinyang, there were 34 clansmen from the Philippines' Jiangxia Huang Clans Association who visited Huangchuan, Xinyang for root-seeking and ancestral sacrifices in April, 1995; root-seeking and Hakka family-visiting delegation with 33 members from Singapore Nanyang Huang Clans Fraternity who visited Huangchuan in April, 1996. On the invitation of Culture Seminar of Xixian Lai Family, clansmen both at home and abroad attended "the Assembly to Commemorate the 3, 118th Anniversary of Shuyinggong's Enfeoffment and Founding of Lai State" in May, 1996. And in April, 1997, 96 members of the Lai Clan Association from Malaysia, Singapore and Hong Kong, Macao and Taiwan of China attended the grand ceremony to commemorate the 3, 119th anniversary of Shuyinggong, the 1st ancestor of Lai clan, as well as Lai Luo's paying homage to his ancestors.

姓氏寻亲活动（固始县文广局秦伟摄影）
Root-seeking Activities of Different Family Names (Photography by Qin Wei, Gushi County Culture and Communication Bureau)

2. 21 世纪初期的根亲活动

进入 21 世纪后，闽台及海外赴河南寻根的活动越来越多，规模也越来越大。

除根亲文化节之外，也有很多宗亲赴固始拜谒寻根。如 2006 年 9 月 5 日，世界苏姓宗亲总会理事长苏用发（印尼）率团来到固始县胡族镇苏岗村祭拜苏老坟——唐代苏奕墓。2006 年 9 月 16 日，海内外黄氏恳亲团一行到固始开展寻根谒祖活动。2009 年 4 月 7 日，台湾开漳圣王庙寻亲团一行 25 人来到固始县寻亲谒祖。2010 年 6 月 24 日，台北景美集应庙高氏河南寻根团一行 19 人，到固始县开展恳亲联谊活动等。

概而言之，固始根亲文化节的举办说明此时期寻根活动有了官方的支持与参与，这就为民间寻根和学界研究营造了有利环境，提供了重要支持。同时，"文化搭台，经济唱戏"的根亲交流形式也为固始县的发展带来了契机，促进了固始县的经济发展。经济发展后，又反哺固始根亲文化建设，形成了良性循环。

2. Root-seeking Activities at the Early 21st Century

After entering the 21st century, root-seeking activities to Henan from Fujian, Taiwan and overseas boomed not only in numbers but in scale.

固始根亲文化节（固始县文广局秦伟摄影）
Gushi Root-seeking Culture Festival (Photography by Qin Wei, Gushi County Culture and Communication Bureau)

Apart from root-seeking culture festival, there were also many clansmen who went to Gushi to pay homage to their roots. For example, on September 5th, 2006, Su Yongfa(Indonesia), Board Chairman of World Su Clan General Association, led a delegation to Sugang Village, Huzu Town, Gushi County to pay homage to Su's ancestral tomb of Su Yi from the Tang Dynasty. On September 16th, 2006, a delegation of Huang family members from home and abroad visited Gushi to pay homage to their ancestors and for their root seeking. On April 7th, 2009, 25 members of the clan tracing delegation from the Temple of Sacred Pioneer of Zhangzhou visited Gushi. On June 24th, 2010, 19 members of Henan root-seeking delegation from the Jiying Temple on Jingmei Street, Taipei, visited Gushi for their family clan reunion activities.

Generally speaking, the holding of the Gushi root-seeking culture festival embarked the way of the official support and participation in root-seeking activities in this period, by which a favorable atmosphere and an important

3. 新时代的根亲活动

新时代的根亲活动延续了之前寻根探亲活动的密度和广度，并且加强了青少年之间的交流。

2011年，国务院正式批复建设中国首个内陆经济改革和对外开放的"中原经济区"，把华夏历史文明传承创新区建设作为中原经济区的五大战略定位之一。河南作为中华姓氏的主要发祥地和起源地，是古代部族融合的核心区域，也是全球华人华侨和客家人的祖根地。近年来，河南省充分挖掘、保护、利用根亲文化资源，通过增加根亲地域资源的文化内涵，唤起华人心中的认同，增强民族向心力和凝聚力。

2012年，"首届全球根亲（客家）文化盛事颁奖大典"在郑州举行，黄帝故里拜祖大典入选世界最具影响力的根亲文化活动，河南有五个市（县）入选"全球华人最向往的十大根亲文化圣地"，分别是新郑、开封、洛阳、淮阳、固始。可见，以河南为中心的根亲文化逐步被全球华人认同，河南成为海外华人心目中寻根谒祖的圣地，有力支撑了华夏历史文明传承创新区建设要打造"一圣地、一高地、三基地"的战略目标和主要任务。

无论是寻根祭祖，参加两岸根亲节庆活动，还是姓氏渊源学术研讨，根亲中原的台湾同胞中，往往以中老年群体为主体，青年人参与较少。进入新时代，两岸有识之士充分利用两岸同文同种独特的血缘纽带、大陆改革开放取得的举世瞩目成果以及中华民族丰富的历史文化遗产，结合青年人知识结构和认识特点，携手组织两岸青年交流交往，已成为两岸根亲文化交流的新亮点。

总而言之，宗亲寻根探亲活动弘扬了中原根亲文化，加强了海内外华人的联系，具有显著的社会价值、经济价值和文化价值。寻根文化作为河南的特色文化，与其他文化相互促进、相辅相成，形成合力，有效地促进了地区经济社会的快速发展。

supporting pillar were created and provided for the folk root-seeking and academic research. Meanwhile, the "culture-based, economy-oriented" root-seeking form of communication has also brought opportunities for the development of Gushi County and promoted her economic development, meaning that a healthy circulation would be achieved for the construction of Gushi root-seeking culture after economic development.

3. Root-seeking Activities in the New Era

Root-seeking activities in the new era inherit the former ones both in density and scope, attaching great importance to the communication between youngsters.

In 2011, the 1st inland zone of opening up and economic reformation—the Central Plains Economic Zone was initiated in China with the official approval of the State Council, which assured the notion of the construction of a Inheritance and Innovation Zone of Chinese Historical Civilization as one of the five strategic positionings of the Central Plains Economic Zone. Henan, as the main birthplace and origin of Chinese surnames, is the core area of ancient tribal integration and the ancestral land of the overseas Chinese and Hakka. In recent years, those root-seeking culture resources have been fully excavated, protected and exploited by Henan Province. By promoting the cultural connotation of root-seeking territorial resources, the sense of self identity was then aroused among all Chinese and it would strengthen the national centripetal force and cohesion of all Chinese around the world.

In 2012, the Award Ceremony of the First Global Root-seeking (Hakka) Cultural Event was held in Zhengzhou, and the Ancestor Worship Ceremony in the hometown of the Yellow Emperor was selected as the most influential root-seeking cultural event in the world. Five cities (counties) in Henan were selected into "the ten most glamorous destinations of root-seeking culture for Chinese in the world", e.g., Xinzheng, Kaifeng, Luoyang, Huaiyang and Gushi. It can be seen that the root-seeking culture centered in Henan has gradually been recognized by all Chinese around the world, and Henan has become a centre for overseas Chinese to seek their ancestral roots and pay homage to their ancestors, strongly catering to the strategic objectives and primary mission of building "a holy land, a highland as well as a base" in the construction of the Inheritance and Innovation

2016 两岸青年中原文化研习营
2016 Cross-Strait Youth Central Plains Culture Study Camp

Zone of Chinese Historical Civilization.

The majority of Taiwan compatriots participating in rooting-seeking activities in the Central Plains, whether they are activities of root-seeking or ancestor worship, cross-Strait root-seeking festivals or academic study of family name tracing, tend to be middle aged and the elderly, but not the youth. When entering the new era, the far-sighted people on both sides of the Strait, making full use of the unique blood ties of the shared culture and ethics, taking advantage of those achievements brought by the reform and opening up policy in Chinese mainland, as well as the rich historical and cultural relics of Chinese nation, organize youth exchanges across the Strait with joined hands by combining the knowledge structure and cognitive feature of young people. These youth exchanges have now become new highlights of cross-Strait cultural communication.

To sum up, the clan root-seeking activities have carried forward the root-seeking culture of the Central Plains and strengthened the contact of Chinese at home and abroad, bearing significant social, economic and cultural value. Root-seeking culture, as the distinctive culture of Henan, promotes and complements other cultures, effectively facilitating the rapid development of regional economy and society.

第三章

水利篇：淮河水利文化

Chapter 3

Water Conservation: Water Conservation Culture

of the Huaihe River

古代淮河与长江、黄河、济水并称"四渎",现代淮河是中国七大江河之一。淮河流域气候温暖,日照充足,雨量充沛,独流入海,水流畅通,曾有"走千走万,不如淮河两岸"的美誉。1194 年,黄河南决,从此长期夺淮入海,淮河便开始了数百年的灾难史。"大雨大灾,小雨小灾,无雨旱灾""要水水不来,恨水水不走",道出了淮河两岸人民的无奈与辛酸。

数千年来,淮河流域的人民怀着对美好生活的向往,一直努力解决水患,也留下了千古传颂的奋斗史。其中,大禹治淮、孙叔敖治淮和"一定要把淮河修好"最为著名。

一、大禹治淮

相传在尧舜时期,中华大地出现了一场大洪水。滔滔洪水淹没了人们生存的家园,吞噬了众多庄稼和农田,使人们生活在危难之中。部落联盟首领尧召集群臣商议对策,大家一致推举鲧去治理洪水。鲧采用修坝堵截的方法,在城池和村庄附近修筑了许多土围子阻挡洪水,让老百姓免受洪灾,但由于当时洪水很大,单纯靠低薄的堤坝并不能阻挡洪流,最终,历时 9 年却没能制服洪水。

后来,部落联盟会议又推举鲧的儿子禹去治水。禹在伯夷、后稷等部落首领的协助下,带领治水队伍,翻山越岭,勘测地形和水势。

通过大量的实地考察,大禹和他的治水队伍改堵为疏,因地制宜,加宽加深河道,把河水依西高东低的地形导流到大海里;同时还在湖泊蓄水,带领百姓在陆地上种植五谷,在水里养鱼虾,通舟楫,各为所用。

大禹还根据山川地理情况,把已经勘测的土地分为九个州,该疏通的疏通,该平整的平整,使大量的荒地变成肥沃的土地。渐渐地,追随协助他们的人越来越多,治水的队伍也越来越大。他们不仅帮助老百姓治理水患,还帮助老百姓发展农桑,大禹在众部落中的威望越来越高。

In ancient China, the Huaihe River, the Yangtze River, the Yellow River, and the Jishui River together were called the "Four Bodies of Water". Nowadays, the Huaihe River is known as one of the seven biggest rivers in China. The climate near the Huaihe River Basin is warm with plenty of sunshine and rain. The Huaihe River continuously flows to the ocean, and people once praised the Huaihe River by saying, "It is better to walk around the Huaihe River than walk thousands of miles in other places." In 1194, the Yellow River overflowed to the south, and started its long-term influx into the Huaihe River by taking it as one of exits to the sea, and hence brought about hundreds of years of natural disasters to the Huaihe River. Residents who lived near the Huaihe River sighed "Heavy rain brings big troubles, small rain brings small troubles, and drought comes when there is no rain." "When we wish it will rain, it would not come; when we wish the rain will stop, it would never stop."

For thousands of years, with the hope of a bright future, the residents near the Huaihe River Basin restlessly tried to solve the problem of the Huaihe River and left the legacy for their hard-working history. "Yu the Great's Taming of the Flood", "Sunshu Ao's Fixing of the Huaihe River", and "Resolutely to Tame the Huaihe River" are the most famous stories of the Huaihe River.

I. Yu the Great's Taming of the Flood

In the period of Yao and Shun, legend goes that a huge flood hit Chinese mainland. The huge influx of water drowned people's homeland and farms and destroyed the harvests and people were living in immense danger. The head of the tribe gathered officials to strategize ways to resolve the issue, and they all agreed to have a man named Gun fix the Huaihe River. His strategy was to build dams around cities and villages to block water. However, the current of the water was so heavy that simply building thin and short barriers could not stop it. In the end, despite working for 9 years, Gun could not successfully stop the overflow of the Huaihe River.

Later, the authorities had another meeting to recommend Gun's son Yu the Great to work on the overflow. Tribe leaders such as Boyi and Houji led Yu and his team to travel around the Huaihe River to check the topography and observe

大禹居外治水 13 年,"三过家门而不入"。因治水有功,大禹成为人们心目中永远的治水英雄,获得中国人民的尊敬,成为中华民族的骄傲。

大禹治水的足迹遍布淮河流域,相关传说也很多,主要有禹锁无支祁和劈山导淮。

周口骆驼岭大禹治水雕塑
The Statue of Yu the Great in Luotuoling of Zhoukou City

1. 禹锁无支祁

淮河的源头桐柏山,有三口淮井,其中一口据说是大禹锁水怪无支祁的地方。大禹为了治水,曾三次来到桐柏山察看水情,每次到达桐柏山都狂风大作,电闪雷鸣,山石号叫,树木惊鸣,到处弥漫着有毒的瘴气,似有一股看不见的暴虐力量阻止了大禹的治水进程,也使当地百姓受到无尽的毒害。

踏遍山川、见多识广的大禹意识到问题的严重性,经多方调查才知道这根本不是简单的瘴气,而是一个名为无支祁的妖怪在作祟。无支祁

the potential flows.

After extensive observations and estimations, Yu and his team changed the strategy from stopping the current to letting the current flow based on geography. This meant that they widened the bank and deepened the watercourse, and let the water flow in its natural course: higher in altitude in the west and lower in altitude in the east. At the same time, they used lakes to store the water and raised fish and shrimp, and instructed the residents to grow grains on the land.

Yu the Great separated the mainland into nine states according to the geography of the mountains and rivers. In each state, he attended to the barren land and made it fertile soil. Gradually, more people joined his team to reorder the Huaihe River. They not only resolved the problems of water overflow, but also improved agriculture. Yu the Great gained a wonderful reputation among the tribes.

Yu spent a total of 13 years fixing the Huaihe River and as a consequence, there left an anecdote of "not entering home when passing by for 3 times". Because of his success, he became a hero to the Chinese people and gained immense respect. Now the whole nation is proud of Yu the Great.

Yu traveled around the Huaihe River Basin and left many heroic myths, two main stories being "Yu the Great Imprisoned Wuzhiqi" and "Yu the Great Chopped the Mountain for Waterflow".

1. Yu the Great Imprisoned Wuzhiqi

The source of the Huaihe River is the Tongbai Mountain, in which there are three wells, one of which is where Yu locked Wuzhiqi, the mythical monster in the water. Yu the Great visited the Tongbai Mountain three times to check the flow of the Huaihe River. Every time he visited, a thunderstorm would hit the Tongbai Mountain and miasma spread everywhere. It seemed like there was an invisible power that stopped Yu the Great from fixing the water, putting residents in great danger.

Yu had seen many cases like this and recognized the seriousness of the issue. He found that it was not as simple as the miasma, but was created by a monster called Wuzhiqi. Dwelling in a deep pool, Wuzhiqi was shaped like a monkey with a small nose and a big forehead. His body was green and he had a white head and

住在一个深潭子中,它"形若猿猴,缩鼻高额,青躯白首,金目血牙,颈伸百尺,力逾九象",还能言善辩,知道江水、淮水各处的深浅,以及地势的高低远近,无论是搏击跳跃,还是快速奔跑,都非常迅捷,常常是眨眼之间就看不见了。它自命为淮涡水神,带领山精水怪长期在淮河流域兴风作浪,祸害百姓。

出生入死治水多年的大禹非常生气,绝不容许无支祁这妖物来造弄水患。于是,双方在桐柏山下展开恶战,大禹先后派童律、乌木由等几位干将出战,都没有成功。大禹又派神将庚申去与无支祁交战。庚申手拿"定海神针",经过三天三夜的鏖战,终于把无支祁制服了。

为了不让无支祁再为祸人间,大禹命人在他鼻孔穿上铜铃铛,脖子挂上大铁链用大锁锁着,然后把他关在淮河南边龟山脚下的深井里。从此,淮河不再泛滥,一直流向大海,桐柏人民得以安居乐业,世代祥和。

2. 劈山导淮

淮河干流有三个峡口,分别是寿县至凤台间的硖山口、怀远的荆山峡口和五河附近的浮山峡口,都是严重阻水的河段。相传,这三个峡口都是大禹开凿的。

淮河从源头桐柏山直泻而下,在进入平原后的第一个峡口——硖山口受阻。大禹来到这里,看了看山势,察了察水情,用规矩左右前后丈量后,认为必须挖开才能将洪水引入东海。于是每天带领治水队伍挖山不止,终于凿开了一条行洪通道。也有传说说是大禹借来天神之鞭,一鞭将整座大山劈成两半。后人把河西那座山称作禹王山,河东那座山称为伯王山。

淮水流出硖山口,进入怀远县,这里有两座山岭——涂山与荆山紧锁河道,形成了淮河上的第二个峡口——荆山峡口。淮水流至荆山的东麓,因为受到荆涂两座山的阻挡,被迫迂回至荆山的西麓,流入涡河,后流入东海。连绵起伏的荆涂山阻挡了大量淮水的流泻,汇集于此的淮

his neck was around a hundred inches. He was extremely strong and his power exceeded nine elephants. Moreover, he was smart and eloquent. Wuzhiqi knew the depth of rivers and the topography well. Whether fighting, jumping or sprinting, he was as fast as the wind. He named himself as the god of the Huaihe River, and led water sprites and monsters to cause many troubles for the residents around the Huaihe River Basin.

Yu was furious at Wuzhiqi. He had spent a very long time fixing the Huaihe River, even risking his life. He could not allow Wuzhiqi to terrorise the people. Yu the Great had a battle with Wuzhiqi at the foot of the Tongbai Mountain. He first dispatched Tonglü, Wumuyou, and other soldiers, but they failed. He then sent Gengshen, who had a magical cudgel, to fight Wuzhiqi. Gengshen spent three days and nights fighting face to face against the monster and succeeded in subduing the monster.

To make sure Wuzhiqi would no longer cause troubles, Yu the Great pinned bells to his nose and locked him in chains. Wuzhiqi was imprisoned in a well under the Turtle Mountain south of the Huaihe River. Since then, overflow never happened to the Huaihe River and water flowed smoothly to the ocean. Residents of the Tongbai Mountain were then able to live happily for many generations.

2. Yu the Great Chopped the Mountain for Waterflow

There are three gorges on the mainstream of the Huaihe River. They are the Xiashan Gorge located between Shouxian and Fengtai County, Jingshan Gorge of Huaiyuan County, and Fushan Gorge of Wuhe County. They are all important bodies of water that help regulate the flow of the water. The legend goes that it is Yu the Great who excavated these gorges.

The Huaihe River springs from the Tongbai Mountain and is interrupted at the first gorge in the plain—Xiashan Gorge. Yu the Great came here to check the topography of the mountains and rivers. Using a ruler and a compass (known as "Yuan" and "Gui") to measure, he concluded that breaking in between the mountain will help the flood run east into the East Sea. He led workers to help dig the mountain day and night, finally opening a route for water to flow. There was also a legend going that Yu the Great borrowed a whip from the god of heaven to hack the mountain in half. Later, descendants named the mountain on

水与涡水严重威胁着当地民众的生命安全。禹带领治水队伍反复勘察，根据水的流向和地形地势，决定将涂山与荆山从中劈开，在两山之间开凿了淮河水道。后人在涂山上修建了规模宏大的禹王宫，刻石记录大禹导淮的英雄事迹。

淮河继续东行，在五河县穿过淮河的第三个峡口——浮山峡口，这是三个峡口中最宽的一峡。峡口南岸是浮山，北岸是潼河山。浮山也叫浮玉山，相传浮山下有仙人洞，每当淮水泛滥时，仙人洞就长高，当洪水退去，仙人洞也随着变低。这座山就像一块碧玉漂浮在淮水中而被称为浮玉，人们怀疑这座山是浮在水上，就把这座山称为浮山。

为了让民众不再受水患困扰，过上安宁的生活，大禹身先士卒，和治水队伍一起栉风沐雨，餐风饮露，克服种种艰难险阻，最终以顽强的毅力和坚持不懈的精神，齐心协力完成了劈山的浩大工程，成功地疏通了水道，疏导了水流，也为后人留下"劈山导淮"的千古佳话。

the west of the river King Yu Mountain, and the mountain on the east of the river King Bo Mountain.

Water from the Huaihe River flowed past Xiashan Gorge and entered Huaiyuan County. There are two mountains in the county—the Tu Mountain and the Jing Mountain. The two mountains together locked the river and formed another gorge called Jingshan Gorge. The water from the Huaihe River flowed to the east of the Jing Mountain, but the obstruction by the Jing Mountain and the Tu Mountain directed the flow of the river west to the Guo River and the East Ocean. However, the two mountains blocked the flow of the Huaihe River, and when the water met the Guo River, the accumulation of water threatened the safety of nearby residents. Yu checked the topography with his team and decided to separate the Tu Mountain and the Jing Mountain by splitting the middle according to the flow of the water. Later, the residents built a magnificent Palace of King Yu on Mountain Tu and engraved his heroic story there on the stone tablet.

The Huaihe River kept flowing east and passed the third gorge at Wuhe County—Fushan Gorge, which is the widest gorge. To the south of it is the Fu Mountain and north, the Tonghe Mountain. The Fu Mountain is also known as the Fuyu Mountain. It is said that there is a fairy cave on the mountain. When the Huaihe River floods, the cave would rise. When the flood subsides, the cave sinks. The mountain is like a jade floating on the Huaihe River, and that is why it is named the Fu Mountain (in English "Floating Mountain").

To rid the flood issues for the residents and allow them to live a better life, Yu the Great, along with his team, had to overcome many troubles such as lack of food and harsh living conditions. Finally, they finished the vast and complicated work of chopping the mountain together with their perseverance. They not only fixed the flow of the Huaihe River, but also left a laudable story of "Chopping the Mountain for Waterflow".

二、孙叔敖治淮

孙叔敖，楚国期思县潘乡（今河南信阳）人，是楚国名相，也是春秋时期的政治家、军事家和水利专家。他一生政绩颇多，尤以水利为最。

孙叔敖雕像（信阳学院冯春晓摄影）
The Statue of Sunshu Ao (Photography by Feng Chunxiao, Xinyang University)

孙叔敖家乡的史河是淮河南岸最大的一条支流。春秋时期，这段河流灾害频发，百姓们流离失所、生计无着。孙叔敖很着急，一心想着怎么样去解决水患。

若干年后，史河流域又遭遇大旱，蝗虫肆虐，大家都明白要种粮食离不开雨水，但是又苦于找不到解决水源的办法。正当大家一筹莫展的时候，孙叔敖说："我有办法，解决干旱并不难，老天没有水，我们可以开渠引水，用合理的方法引附近的水源灌溉田地。干旱不足为虑，请

II. Sunshu Ao's Fixing of the Huaihe River

Sunshu Ao, who was originally from Pan Village, Qisi County (present Xinyang, Henan), was a famous government official, military strategist, and water conservation expert in Chu State during the Spring and Autumn Period. He has numerous achievements, especially in water conservation.

The Shi River in Sunshu Ao's hometown was the largest tributary of the Huaihe River to the south. In the Spring and Autumn Period, disasters hit the Shi River frequently and the residents nearby had to leave their hometown and were deprived of basic necessities of life. Sunshu Ao was very worried and wanted to solve this problem.

Years later, locusts wreaked havoc in the Shi River Basin due to the serious drought in the area. People knew that the harvests could not survive without water, but they could not find a source. When no one could come up with a solution, Sunshu Ao then proposed, "It is not hard to end the drought. If it is not raining, we can open the canals to lead the nearest water into the fields." However, people did not believe him. They judged him as too ambitious and unrealistic, because they thought there weren't any water resources.

Initially, Sunshu Ao was upset because nobody believed or supported him. Despite people's doubts, he did not give up, "Even if it is only me, I have to fix the problem." He sold his properties to buy supplies to build a dam. After a long period of exhausting work, he successfully built a dam, but he was too tired so he passed out one day. A senior official, Yuqiu Zi, passed by and helped him get up. Yuqiu Zi asked Sunshu Ao what he was doing and why he collapsed. Sunshu Ao told Yuqiu Zi that although he had solutions to help ease the drought in this area, nobody trusted him because he was too young and they believed he could not accomplish it by himself. Sunshu Ao said, "I will continue doing this to fix the water even though it is only myself because I want to prove my ability to them."

Yuqiu Zi was deeply touched by his perseverance and provided him with money, supplies, and manual labor that Sunshu Ao needed for building the water conservation system. With Yuqiu Zi's help, Sunshu Ao finally built the very first large irrigation system "Qisibei". This system and irrigation area are located in the area around the present Huaibin, Gushi and Shangcheng. The system utilized

大家相信我。"可是村民并不认同他,都说他年轻好高骛远,干旱一来哪里有水源,一番嘲讽后,大家就离开了。

孙叔敖见没有人相信、支持他,很伤心。但是面对别人的讥诮,他没有放弃,暗暗发誓:"就算只有我,我也要治水。"他变卖家产,筹集物资,挑石头,建堤坝,功夫不负有心人,终于修好了一截堤坝,但他也累得头晕眼花昏倒在地。正好楚国令尹虞丘子路过,把他扶起来,问他在做些什么,怎么会落到独自一人晕倒的地步。他说:"这里常有干旱,我有灌溉之法,但是因为太过年轻别人都不信我,大家都认为凭我一己之力不可能把水治好。所以哪怕独自一人倾家荡产我也要造好堤坝,解决旱情,证明给他们看。"

虞丘子深受感动,很快替孙叔敖解决了治水的财力、物力和人力问题。在虞丘子的帮助下,孙叔敖最终建成了中国最早的大型灌溉工程——期思陂。该工程和灌区位于今河南淮滨、固始、商城一带,在今淮河支流白露河、灌河通过决河引水,顺势而下,充分利用废旧河道和两岸的湖沼洼地,做到涝时能蓄,旱时能灌。

公元前597年,楚庄王把芍陂工程交给孙叔敖负责。孙叔敖利用这里天然的洼地和湖泊,在四周筑堤蓄水,开有五座引水门,用石制闸门控制水量,开渠引水,自流灌溉,并引导百姓开发稻田,不仅天旱有水灌田,还避免了水多洪涝成灾。后来又在西南开了一道子午渠,使得芍陂达到了灌田万顷的规模。孙叔敖兴修水利,开创了中国农业灌溉的先河。他励精图治,助楚国成为五霸之一的强国,他也因而成为一代名相。

芍陂水利工程作为首座大型塘堰灌溉工程,至今仍然在发挥作用,被称为"淮河水利之冠"。

the burst of the embankment of the tributaries Bailu River and Guan River to lead the water flow downwards, and by making full use of the abandoned river channels and the lakes and swamps on both sides of the river, the project achieved the function of storing water during floods and irrigating during droughts.

In 597 BC, Emperor Zhuang of the Chu State handed over the Quebei project to Sunshu Ao. Sunshu Ao made use of the natural depressions and lakes to build embankments around the river to store water. He built five water diversion gates, used stone gates to control the amount of water, opened canals to divert water for artesian flow irrigation, and guided the people to develop paddy fields to guarantee there was water during drought and keeping safe in a flood. Later, the Meridian Canal was dug in the southwest, making Quebei reach a scale of 10,000 hectares of irrigated fields. Sunshu Ao built a water conservancy and created a precedent for agricultural irrigation in China. He worked hard to govern and helped the Chu State become one of the five hegemons, and he also became a famous figure of the generation.

As the first large-scale pond and weir irrigation project, the Quebei Water Conservancy Project is still in use and is known as the "First-rate Project of the Huaihe Water Conservancy Ones".

世界灌溉工程遗产——芍陂水利工程（信阳学院冯春晓摄影）
The Statue of the Quebei Water Conservancy Project (Photography by Feng Chunxiao, Xinyang University)

三、一定要把淮河修好

《一定要把淮河修好》图书
Book of *Resolutely to Tame the Huaihe River*

历史上，各朝代虽然对淮河进行过局部治理，但都没能从根本上解决水患。而新中国治淮则是在国家统一规划和指导下进行的。

1950年6月至7月，河南、安徽两省交界区突降大暴雨。持续了半个多月的暴雨，在淮北地区引发了大洪水，大批房屋被冲毁，大片土地被淹没，仅河南和安徽两地淮河全流域就有1300多万人受灾。毛泽东高度重视淮河流域的灾情，在7月20日至9月21日两个月的时间内，就治淮问题连续作了4次批示。10月14日，中央人民政府政务院发布《关于治理淮河的决定》，确定了"蓄泄兼筹，以达根治之目的"的治淮总方针，揭开了淮河治理历史的新篇章。淮河成为新中国第一条全面系统治理的大河。

1951年5月，毛泽东主席发出"一定要把淮河修好"的指示，更加坚定了人们治水的决心。1957年冬，这一阶段的治淮工程基本完成，

III. Resolutely to Tame the Huaihe River

Historically, although a lot of dynasties have carried out partial control of the Huaihe River, they have not been able to solve the root problem of the flood. The governance of the Huaihe River after the establishment of the PRC was carried out under unified planning and guidance.

From June to July, 1950, heavy rain fell suddenly between the border of Henan and Anhui provinces. The heavy rain lasted for more than half a month, causing major floods in the northern of the Huaihe River area. The floods washed away houses as well as completely submerged large patches of land. More than 13 million residents were affected in the entire region of the Huaihe River Basin in Henan and Anhui provinces. Mao Zedong paid a lot of attention to the disaster in these areas. From July 20th to September 21st of 1950, he made four consecutive instructions on the management of the Huaihe River. On October 14th, the Government Affairs Council of the Central People's Government issued the *Resolution on Governing the Huaihe River*, which ascertained the general policy of "storing and discharging to achieve the purpose of radical governance", opening a new chapter in the history of the Huaihe River governance. The Huaihe River became the first large river under comprehensive and systematic governance in the PRC.

In May 1951, President Mao Zedong issued an instruction of "Resolutely to Tame the Huaihe River", which reinforced people's determination to solve the problems with the river. In the winter of 1957, the Huaihe River control project was periodically completed. Among them, five large reservoirs, respectively the Baisha Reservoir, the Shimantan Reservoir, the Banqiao Reservoir, the Boshan Reservoir, and the Nanwan Reservoir, were built in Henan Province in the upper reaches of the Huaihe River. Four large reservoirs, namely the Foziling Reservoir, the Xianghongdian Reservoir, the Meishan Reservoir, and the Mozitan Reservoir were built in Anhui Province in the middle reaches of the Huaihe River. Among them, the Meishan Reservoir and the Xianghongdian Reservoir are the two largest. The construction of these reservoirs played a crucial role in resolving the flooding of the Huaihe River.

其中淮河上游的河南省修建了白沙水库、石漫滩水库、板桥水库、薄山水库和南湾水库等 5 座大型水库；淮河中游安徽修建了佛子岭水库、响洪甸水库、梅山水库和磨子潭水库等 4 座库容较大的水库，其中梅山水库和响洪甸水库是淮河流域最大的两座水库。这些水库的修建对解决淮河的水患起到了至关重要的作用。

1. 白沙水库

白沙水库坐落在河南登封与禹州市的交界处，始建于 1951 年 3 月，1953 年 8 月竣工，因为大坝紧靠禹州花石镇白沙北村而得名。

白沙水库建成以后，先后修建了四条干渠，即南干渠、北干渠、东干渠和新北干渠，这些水利设施的兴建，极大地增加了灌溉的面积，也极大地促进了当地农业经济的发展。白沙水库不仅发挥了防洪、灌溉、保护生态、水产养殖等功能，还成为观光览胜的旅游区。

2. 石漫滩水库

石漫滩水库坐落在河南省平顶山舞钢市境内，1951 年 7 月建成，是新中国成立后淮河流域上游兴建的第一座大型水库，被誉为"淮河明珠"。

1975 年 8 月，一场特大暴雨造成的洪水洪峰流量超过水库设计标准的数倍，同时又因为运行管理的失误，导致洪水漫顶溃坝失事。1993 年 9 月水库动工复建，1998 年 1 月投入使用。水库的复建极大地改善了舞钢市的自然环境，使其山、水、林、城融为一体。

建于 1998 年的石漫滩水库国家森林公园，2001 年被批准为首批国家水利风景区。石漫滩水利风景区展示了石漫滩水库的兴建、溃决、复建的历史及发展过程。景区里有复建后气势雄伟的治淮第一坝，有 1975 年 8 月大洪水冲毁的大坝遗迹，还有讲述大禹治水故事的 30 米巨幅长卷。作为我国唯一保留的大水毁后的大坝和复建后的大坝同时并存的水库，

1. The Baisha Reservoir

The Baisha Reservoir is located at the intersection of Dengfeng and Yuzhou City of Henan Province. It began to be built in March, 1951 and was completed in August, 1953. It is named due to its proximity to Baisha North Village, Huashi Town, Yuzhou City.

After the Baisha Reservoir was completed, four main canals were built: the South Main Canal, the North Main Canal, the East Main Canal, and the Xinbei Main Canal. The construction of these water conservation facilities greatly increased the irrigation area and as well strikingly promoted the local agriculture and economy. Baisha Reservoir not only has roles in flood control, irrigation, ecological protection, aquaculture, etc., but also is a tourist attraction.

2. The Shimantan Reservoir

The Shimantan Reservoir is located in Wugang City, Pingdingshan, Henan Province. It was completed in July, 1951. It is the first large-scale reservoir built in the upper reaches of the Huaihe River Basin after the founding of the People's Republic of China. It is known as the "Pearl of the Huaihe River".

In August, 1975, heavy rain caused the flow of the river to exceed the capacity of the reservoir. Problems in operation and management combined, resulted in the collapse of the dam. The reconstruction of the reservoir started in September, 1993, and was completed in January, 1998. The reconstruction of the reservoir has greatly improved the natural environment of Wugang City, integrating its mountains, water, forest and city.

The Shimantan Reservoir National Forest Park, built in 1998, was approved as the first batch of National Water Conservancy Scenic Spot in 2001. The Shimantan Water Conservancy Scenic Area shows the history of the construction, collapse and reconstruction of the Shimantan Reservoir. In the scenic spot, there is the majestic First Dam of Taming the Huaihe River after its reconstruction, the remains of the dam destroyed by the flood, and a huge 30-meter-long scroll that tells the story of Yu the Great's flood control. As the only remaining reservoir in the country where both the dam destroyed by the flood and the dam after reconstruction coexist, the Shimantan Reservoir serves as a warning for future generations to always be alert.

石漫滩水库有极强的警示作用，警世后人时刻保持警惕。

3. 薄山水库

薄山水库又叫薄山湖，坐落在驻马店市确山县城南 20 公里处，是溱头河上游的大型山谷水库。

薄山水库在发挥着防洪、灌溉作用的同时，也在生态保护、旅游观光等方面发挥着重要的作用。水库库区现已开发为国家级水利风景区——薄山湖风景区，景区内有虎啸峰、野猪岭、卢王寨遗址、翠竹溪、骆驼峰、龙女潭、将军壁、灵龟岛、猴儿崖等著名景观，因山水环绕、景色优美而被称为"中原漓江"。

4. 南湾水库

南湾水库坐落在淮河支流浉河上，在信阳市西南 8.5 公里处。南湾湖大坝距市区中心 7 公里，隶属于南湾风景管理区，是新中国成立后首批兴建的大型治淮骨干工程之一。南湾水库的修建始于 1952 年 12 月，至 1955 年 11 月建成。

南湾水库大坝（信阳学院冯春晓摄影）

The Dam of the Nanwan Reservoir (Photography by Feng Chunxiao, Xinyang University)

3. The Boshan Reservoir

The Boshan Reservoir, also known as the Boshan Lake, is located 20 kilometers south of Queshan County, Zhumadian City. It is a large valley reservoir in the upper reaches of the Zhentou River.

The Boshan Reservoir not only has the roles of flood control and irrigation, but also plays an important part in ecological protection, tourism and other aspects. The reservoir area has been developed into a national-level water conservancy scenic spot—Boshan Lake Scenic Area, and the famous scenic spots include Tiger Growling Peak, Wild Boar Ridge, Luwangzhai Site, Cuizhu Stream, Camel Peak, Longnü Pool, General Wall, Turtle Island and Monkey Cliff. Boshan Lake Scenic Area is then known as the "Lijiang River (one of the best scenic spots of mountains and waters in Guilin, Guangxi) in the Central Plains" because of the beautiful scenery surrounded by mountains and rivers.

4. The Nanwan Reservoir

The Nanwan Reservoir is located on the Shihe River, a tributary of the Huaihe River, 8.5 kilometers southwest of Xinyang City. The Nanwan Lake Dam is 7 kilometers away from the downtown area. It belongs to the Nanwan Scenic Management Zone and is one of the 1st batch large scale and key Huaihe governance projects built after the founding of the PRC. The construction of the Nanwan Reservoir began in December, 1952 and was completed in November, 1955.

The Nanwan Reservoir is an irreplaceable landmark for Xinyang people. It guarantees downstream agricultural irrigation and drinking water to the residents of the Xinyang urban area. As time goes, the functions of the Nanwan Reservoir are gradually changing, integrating power generation, aquaculture and tourism. The Nanwan Lake has become a dazzling pearl embedded in the upper reaches of

南湾水库对于信阳人而言,是不可替代的存在。它是下游农业灌溉的保障,也是信阳市区饮用水的保证。随着时代的发展,南湾水库的功能在逐步发生变化,在承担着防洪、灌溉重任的同时,也集发电、水产养殖和旅游为一体,库区"南湾湖"已成为镶嵌在淮河上游的一颗明珠。

5. 梅山水库

梅山水库坐落在素有"红军故乡、将军摇篮"之誉的安徽省金寨县县城南端,始建于 1954 年 3 月,1956 年 4 月建成,是我国自主设计、自行施工兴建的新中国第二座连拱坝大型水库。这座钢筋混凝土连拱坝全长 443.5 米,坝高 88.24 米,是当时世界上最高的连拱坝。

梅山水库是集防洪、灌溉、发电、航运、水产养殖和旅游等于一体的大型水利枢纽工程,其景点众多的"绿色"旅游资源与金寨县"红色"旅游资源交相辉映,吸引着无数中外游客,被水利部评为国家级水利风景区。

6. 响洪甸水库

响洪甸水库坐落在安徽省六安市金寨县,是淮河支流西淠河上的一座大型水利工程。响洪甸水库的修建始于 1956 年 4 月,至 1958 年 7 月竣工。

响洪甸水库大坝是我国自主设计、自主施工的第一座等半径同圆心混凝土重力拱坝。库区利用独特的自然环境,在山区大力发展林业,有闻名的齐山翠眉和六安瓜片等名茶。库区还大力发展渔业,取得了很大的经济效益。另外,库区还充分开发、利用水资源,建设了响洪甸混合式抽水蓄能电站——安徽省第一座抽水蓄能电站,极大地提高了响洪甸水库综合发电和防洪抗旱的能力。

the Huaihe River.

5. The Meishan Reservoir

The Meishan Reservoir is located at the southern end of Jinzhai County, Anhui Province, a county known as "the hometown of the Red Army and the cradle of Generals". It was built in March, 1954 and completed in April, 1956. It is the second large multi-arch dam reservoir designed and constructed independently in the PRC. With a total length of 443.5 meters and a height of 88.24 meters, this reinforced concrete multi-arch dam was the highest one in the world at that time.

The Meishan Reservoir is a large-scale water conservation project integrating flood control, irrigation, power generation, shipping, aquaculture and tourism. Its numerous "green" tourism (nature) resources and Jinzhai County's "red" tourism (revolution history) resources complement each other, attracting countless Chinese and foreign tourists. It was rated as a national water conservancy scenic spot by the Ministry of Water Resources.

6. The Xianghongdian Reservoir

The Xianghongdian Reservoir is located in Jinzhai County, Liu'an City, Anhui Province. It is a large-scale water conservation project on the Xipi River, a tributary of the Huaihe River. The construction of the Xianghongdian Reservoir began in April, 1956 and was completed in July, 1958.

The Xianghongdian Reservoir Dam is the first concentric concrete gravity arch dam with equal radius designed and constructed in China. Taking advantage of the unique natural environment, the reservoir area strives to boost forestry in the mountainous area. There are famous teas such as Qishan Cuimei and Liu'an Guapian. The reservoir area has also made great efforts to develop fishery, adding notable economic benefits. In addition, the reservoir area has also fully developed and utilized water resources and has built the Xianghongdian hybrid pumped-storage power station, the first pumped-storage power station in Anhui Province, which has greatly improved its comprehensive power generation, flood control and drought relief capabilities.

7. 出山店水库

出山店水库是国家大型水库,从 1953 年开始设计,40 多年来两次开工、两次停工,1999 年再度"出山"。出山店水库规划坝址在淮河干流的信阳市浉河区游河乡出山店村。坝址以上至淮河发源地河道长 100 公里,水库控制流域面积 2900 平方公里,总库容 12.51 亿立方米。规划主坝长 3690.57 米(其中混凝土坝长 429.57 米,土坝长 3261 米),最大坝高 34.5 米,设计灌溉面积 50 万亩,水电装机 2900 千瓦,工程投资约 98.696 亿元,是一座以防洪、灌溉、供水为主,结合发电、水产养殖、旅游、航运等综合开发利用的国家大型水库。

水库的建成是对沿淮人民的关爱,为治淮工作写下浓墨重彩的一笔,永远载入治淮历史史册。

在"一定要把淮河修好"指示精神的激励下,新中国几代人筚路蓝缕、励精图治,最终在淮河流域建成了集水库、堤防、行蓄洪区、水闸、分洪河道、湖泊和防汛指挥系统等于一体的较为完善的防洪抗旱减灾工程体系。到 2021 年,淮河流域已经建成了 6000 多座大小不等的水库,它们于新时代继续在环境、经济、文化、社会等方面发挥着不可替代的作用。

出山店水库(信阳学院冯春晓摄影)

The Chushandian Reservoir (Photography by Feng Chunxiao, Xinyang University)

7. The Chushandian Reservoir

The Chushandian Reservoir is a large-scale national reservoir. The design began in 1953. In more than 40 years, it was started twice and stopped twice. In 1999, the construction was started again. The planned dam site of the Chushandian Reservoir is Chushandian Village, Youhe Town, Shihe District, Xinyang City, on the main stream of the Huaihe River. It covers 100 kilometers from the dam site to the source of the Huaihe River, and the reservoir controls a drainage area of 2,900 square kilometers with a total storage capacity of 1.251 billion cubic meters. The planned main dam is 3690.57 meters long (including 429.57 meters long for the concrete dam and 3261 meters long for the earth dam), the maximum dam height is 34.5 meters, the designed irrigation area is 500,000 *mu*, its installed hydropower capacity is 2,900 kilowatts, and the project investment is about 9.8696 billion *yuan*. It is a national level large-scale reservoir designed largely for flood control, irrigation and water supply combined with the comprehensive development and utilization of power generation, aquaculture, tourism, and shipping.

The completion of the reservoir was a service for the people along the Huaihe River, and a masterpiece for the conservation of the Huaihe River, which will be forever recorded in the annals of history.

Inspired by the spirit of the instruction of "Resolutely to Tame the Huaihe River", several generations of people in China have endured hardships and made painstaking efforts, and have built reservoirs, dams, flood storage areas, sluices, flood diversion channels, lakes and flood control command systems in the Huaihe River Basin, finally perfecting flood control and drought relief engineering system. By 2021, more than 6,000 reservoirs of various sizes had been built in the Huaihe River Basin, and they will continue to play an irreplaceable role in the areas of environment, economy, culture, and society in the new era.

第四章

饮食篇：信阳茶和信阳菜

Chapter 4

Diets: Xinyang Tea and Cuisine

一、信阳茶：信阳毛尖

1. 信阳与信阳毛尖

信阳市位于河南省南部、淮河上游、大别山北麓，东邻安徽，南接湖北，承东启西，连南贯北，素有三省通衢之称。信阳市地处南北气候过渡带，属亚热带向暖温带过渡区，全市年均降雨量1200毫米左右，年平均气温15.1℃，日照充足，雨量丰沛，山水相依，泉明林翠，享有"江南北国，北国江南"的美誉。

信阳是茶的故乡，茶是信阳的象征，是信阳市的"金名片"。信阳地处我国茶叶生产的江北茶区，和江南、华南、西南茶区相比，茶园面积和茶叶产量不高，但茶叶质量却在全国名列前茅，是我国优质茶叶的主产区之一。"信阳毛尖"是传统的中国十大名茶之一，品牌知名度较高。

信阳与信阳毛尖（信阳学院冯春晓摄影）

Xinyang and Its Green Tea—Xinyang Maojian (Photography by Feng Chunxiao, Xinyang University)

信阳种茶始于东周，名于唐，兴于宋，盛于清，历史悠久，茶文化源远流长，是古代著名的淮南茶区。唐代茶圣陆羽在《茶经》中评价，"淮南以光州（今信阳）上……"；宋代大文豪苏东坡曾惊叹"淮南茶，信阳第一……"。信阳毛尖以外形细圆紧直、色泽翠绿、白毫显露、内质汤色嫩绿明亮、滋味鲜爽回甘、香气馥郁持久而享誉海内外，屡获殊荣。

I. Xinyang Green Tea: Xinyang Maojian

1. Xinyang and Xinyang Maojian

Xinyang City is located in the south of Henan Province, along the upper reaches of the Huaihe River and north side of the Dabie Mountain. The city is famous for its central location, bordering Anhui Province to the east, Hubei to the south, and it is the pivot both of north and south, and east and west. Xinyang is at the transitioning area between Northern and Southern China, which is categorized as a subtropical zone. The annual precipitation is about 1,200 millimeters, and the average annual temperature is 15.1°C. Therefore, Xinyang is also known as "the North in Jiangnan, Jiangnan in the North" for its abundance in natural resources, including sunshine, forests, and water.

Xinyang is the hometown of green tea, while green tea is the symbol of the city and her sparkling identity card. As one of the main tea producing districts of China, Xinyang is located in the Jiangbei district, and the annual tea production quantity and acreage is relatively low compared with other districts such as the Jiangnan, Huanan, and Xi'nan. In terms of quality, however, the Jiangbei district ranks highly. The Xinyang Maojian tea, as a well-known tea brand, is recognized as one of the "Ten Best Traditional Chinese Teas".

The tradition of tea planting in Xinyang started from the Eastern Zhou Dynasty, and was popularized and transformed throughout the following dynasties until modern times. Xinyang tea was loved by the public and praised by many well-known Chinese poets, including the "Tea Saint" Lu Yu of the Tang Dynasty and Su Dongpo of the Song Dynasty. The Xinyang Maojian leaves are in thin and round shape, firmly rolled with pointy edges. The leaves usually have a dark green color covered with white leaf hair that is dried during the production process. After brewing, the Maojian tea appears to be light green with a thick yet refreshing taste and a long-lasting aftertaste. Its unique appearance and delicious taste attract worldwide attention and popularity.

In 1915, at the Panama International Tea Exposition, Xinyang Maojian won the gold medal, and was awarded as the top ten famous tea of China in 1958. In 1990, it won the first prize in the National Green Tea Competition. Later in

淮南茶信阳第一（信阳学院冯春晓摄影）

Xinyang Tea, Topping the Green Teas of Huainan Area (Photography by Feng Chunxiao, Xinyang University)

1915 年，信阳毛尖获巴拿马万国博览会金奖；1958 年，被评为全国十大名茶；1990 年，在全国绿茶评比中，以最高分获得中国质量奖金奖；1999 年，获得昆明世界园艺博览会金奖。同时，"信阳毛尖"茶先后获得原产地地理标志产品、生态原产地保护产品，"信阳毛尖传统采制技艺"成功入选国家非物质文化遗产项目名录，信阳市被中国林业生态发展促进会授予"中国毛尖之都"称号，信阳茶文化节被评为"中国十大茶事样板"之一。2019 年 4 月，经浙江大学 CARD 中国农业品牌研究中心评估，信阳毛尖品牌价值以 65.31 亿元连续 10 年位居全国前三位。

2. 信阳茶事典故

（1）村姑·画眉·茶树

在信阳市浉河边的茶之韵广场上，有一尊名叫"茶姐画眉"的雕塑十分引人注目。游人来到这里，总爱站在茶姐的雕像前仔细端祥，回味着那虽然时间遥远但仍被历史保鲜的故事。

传说很久之前，信阳大山里住着一位善良的村姑，她看到父老乡亲都爱患一种叫"疲劳瘆"的疾病，十分焦急。她听说古代有一位叫神农

1999, Xinyang Maojian again won the gold medal in the World Horticultural Exposition at Kunming. Furthermore, Xinyang Maojian was recognized as the "Origin Geographical Indication Product" and "Ecological Origin Protecting Product". The Traditional Picking and Production Process of Xinyang Maojian was placed in the list of the National Intangible Cultural Heritage. At the same time, Xinyang City was named as the "Capital of Maojian" and Xinyang Tea Culture Festival was rated as one of the "Top Ten Tea Culture Events in China". A research study conducted by Zhejiang University in April, 2019 suggested that the Xinyang Maojian brand, with the value of 6.531 billion *yuan*, ranked among the top three in the value of public tea brands in China for over ten years.

国家级非物质文化传承项目信阳毛尖制作工艺传承人周祖宏（右）在炒茶
（信阳学院冯春晓摄影）
Zhou Zuhong, on the Right, the Heir of Xinyang Maojian Tea Art, Is Stir-frying Tea
(Photography by Feng Chunxiao, Xinyang University)

2. Tales of Xinyang Tea

(1) The Village Girl, The Huamei Bird (Wood Thrush) and The Tea Tree

In the Chazhiyun Square, along the Shi River in Xiangyang City, there stands a statue of the "Tea Sister Huamei". This is a famous tourist spot where people can admire the "Tea Sister" and be in retrospect the remote but perfuming history of tea.

Legend went that there lived a kind and brave village girl in the mountains of Xinyang long time ago. She noticed that many villagers had been infected with

氏的人，在西南方向找到了一种能治百病的树叶，便决心前去寻访这种宝树。

不畏艰险的村姑，向西南方向爬过了九十九座高山，又越过了九十九条大河，结果饥饿和劳累使她也患上了"疲劳痧"，病倒在一片树林边。这时已在天上做了神仙的神农氏降临在村姑的身边，他从一棵树上摘下几片树叶，让村姑咀嚼吃下，村姑很快就苏醒痊愈了。神农氏指着那棵树告诉村姑，这种树叫茶树，可以治愈"疲劳痧"病，但种子必须尽快种到土里才能成活。他提出先把村姑变成一只画眉鸟，这样可以尽快把种子衔回去，等茶树长成之后，她就会变回原来的模样，但在茶树长成之前，不能唱歌，也不能大笑，否则就无法再变回去。村姑愉快地答应了神农氏的要求。

小画眉衔着茶籽回到了家乡，把茶籽迅速种到了土里。很快，那茶籽就生根发芽，并日益长大。这时小画眉忘记了神农氏的嘱咐，高兴地唱起歌来，这一唱就使她再也变不回去了，永远地成了一只小画眉。而那发芽的茶籽也很快长成了茶树。如今在信阳漫山遍野的茶树林里，常见有一种尖嘴大眼、羽毛美丽的画眉鸟，经常落在茶树上，唱着好听的歌儿，啄吃树上的害虫，人们说那就是村姑变成的画眉鸟。

（2）陆羽访茶入信阳

史载，陆羽曾下榻古光州固始紫阳洞，被这里的山光水色、泉甘茶香所迷恋，一住就是数年。他平日与崇佛寺、太阳庙、观音洞等寺庙里的大师为友，互相唱酬；白天赏茶、采茶，晚间谈诗品茶，探讨茶事，著书立说，学识大进。他为了考察淮南茶区，复东出舒州，南下黄州，北上寿州，再回紫阳洞，写出《淮南茶初考》草稿。陆羽走后，山民为了纪念他对淮南茶的贡献，在紫阳洞中增设了他的神位，定清明节为敬茶神节。信阳民间至今保留有"清明采新茶，试新火"的雅事。

the disease "Pilaosha" which was caused by overworking. Worried for the villagers, the girl decided to risk southwestward hunting the magic tree with diseases-proof leaves, which were believed found by the alleged Shennong.

Brave and determined, she climbed mountains after mountains and crossed rivers after rivers. Unfortunately, due to hunger and exhaustion she was also caught by the disease of "Pilaosha" and collapsed to the ground unconsciously. Shennong, the heavenly god, appeared and healed the girl by feeding her a leaf from a nearby tree. Shennong told the girl that this leaf came from a tea tree which could cure "Pilaosha". The tree seeds, however, should be planted as soon as possible in order for the tree to survive. Therefore, Shennong suggested turning the girl into a Huamei bird, a type of songbird, which travels faster in the wild. Shennong said the spell would be broken once the tree grew up, but she could not sing or laugh while the tree was still growing or she would remain as a Huamei bird forever. The girl happily agreed to the terms and returned to the village.

茶姐画眉（信阳学院冯葆炜摄影）
Tea Sister Huamei (Photography by Feng Baowei, Xinyang University)

茶圣陆羽（信阳学院冯春晓摄影）
"Tea Saint" Lu Yu (Photography by Feng Chunxiao, Xinyang University)

（3）苏轼游申留佳话

宋代大文豪苏东坡也是个"饮君子"，写了不少茶诗、茶词。在诗中，他把茶叶比作佳人，赋予茶叶佳人的神韵。他喝遍了全国的名茶，当来到信阳，品茗了信阳茶后，连声感叹"淮南茶，信阳第一""品不在浙、闽之下"。

宋代大文豪苏东坡（信阳学院冯春晓摄影）
Su Dongpo, Eminent Writer in the Song Dynasty (Photography by Feng Chunxiao, Xinyang University)

The little Huamei bird flew back home as fast as she could and planted the seed at once. As Shengnong said, the tree grew fast and strong with the great care of little Huamei. However, she forgot about the spell and started to sing joyfully because of the tree's growth. As a result, she remained as a Huamei bird for the rest of her life. The tea tree eventually became a full-grown tree and spread its seeds along the mountains and forests of Xinyang. In the woods nowdays, villagers often spot a songbird flying and singing between the tea trees and they believe she is the village girl, the Tea Sister.

(2) Lu Yu and the Xiangyang Tea

The ancient Chinese writer Lu Yu, known as the "Tea Master" or "Tea Saint", once visited the Ziyang Cave in present-day southern Henan. Amazed by the natural scenery and the local tea art, Lu stayed in the village for many years. He became close with the monks from the Chongfo Temple, the Sun Temple, and the Guanyin Cave. Drinking tea, picking tea, and analyzing writings about tea art became their daily routine. In order to study the entire Huainan tea district, Lu traveled to the present-day Henan, Hubei, and Anhui provinces. After his exploration, he returned to Ziyang Cave where he drafted the *Initial Analysis of the Huainan Tea*. After Lu Yu left the village, the residents honoured his contribution by placing Lu's memorial tablet in the Ziyang Cave and worshiping the "Tea Saint" on every Qingming Festival, the Tomb Sweeping Day. The tradition of savoring new tea brewed by new fire (out of a taboo that forbidding the use of fire 2 days before the Qingming Festival) is still preserved today.

信阳茶廉广场上的《茶经》论廉（信阳学院冯春晓摄影）
On Honesty and Uprightness in the *Book of Tea* on the Chalian Square in Xinyang City
(Photography by Feng Chunxiao, Xinyang University)

（4）毛主席给信阳茶农寄茶钱

1956年初夏，信阳浉河区董家河车云山村夏复新、席本荣等7位村民亲自上山采摘、烘焙、杀青，使用8道工序，精制出2斤信阳毛尖，上写"北京毛主席收"几个字，寄往北京。一个月后，收到了中央办公厅的回信，信中附了茶叶款和有关种茶资料。

3. 信阳茶馆及茶艺表演

（1）信阳茶馆

饮茶不仅满足身体需要，也为国人雅趣。茶馆是人们饮茶的重要场所。中国的茶馆萌芽于西晋，成型于唐代。根据唐代封演所著《封氏闻见录》描述的长安饮茶风气，"不问道俗，投钱取饮"，可见唐代时茶馆已经十分普遍。信阳的茶馆业起于何时，现无定论，一般认为，明代信阳城内已有茶馆业经营。到了清代，信阳城内的大街小巷茶馆棋布，许多茶馆的大门书有"客至心常热，人走茶不凉""浉河中心水，车云顶上茶"等对联，用以招徕茶客。随着人们生活水平的提高，信阳各种风格的茶馆、茶艺馆、茶餐厅鳞次栉比，坐落于信阳市浉河岸畔的"茶文化一条街"有30多家茶庄、茶艺馆，每天都吸引着大量的茶客。

（2）茶艺表演

茶艺表演（亦称茶道表演）是一门艺术，是茶事与文化的完美结合。信阳茶艺表演博采众长，丰富多彩，展示了信阳茶婀娜多姿、清香馥郁的内在品质和内涵丰厚、高雅灵秀的茶文化底蕴。近年来，信阳茶艺表演不仅配合地方经济建设、重大节日随时演出，而且还走进北京、上海、郑州、武汉等大都市，登上大雅之堂，受到广泛的赞誉，赢得一片喝彩。

(3) Su Shi the Poet and Xinyang Tea

Su Dongpo, one of the most well-known poets in Chinese history, was a "teaholic" and wrote numerous tea poems. In his poems, Su liked to personify tea as beauties, bestowing tea with beauties' charm and personality. Having tasted teas from almost all parts of China, he finally came to Xinyang and after tasting the famous Xinyang tea, he was convinced that Xinyang had the best tea out of all Huainan tea districts and the tea was not at all inferior to those of Fujian and Zhejiang provinces.

(4) Chairman Mao and His Tea Order

In the early summer of 1956, seven villagers from southern Henan, including Xia Fuxin and Xi Benrong, picked tea leaves from their local mountains. They made about 1 kg of Xinyang Maojian with the eight steps process and mailed it directly to Chairman Mao Zedong in Beijing. A month later, they received a letter and a payment for the tea and at the same time some tea planting reference books from the Central Government.

3. Xinyang Teahouse and Tea Art Performance

(1) Xinyang Teahouse

Tea drinking not only provides the necessary supplements for people's bodies, but also serves as the elegant way of entertainment in Chinese culture. Teahouses, the most common places to drink tea, appeared as early in Western Jin, and became well established in the Tang Dynasty. According to *The Record of the Feng*, a book that records life in the Tang Dynasty, people from all walks are welcome to enjoy tea in these houses. Although the origination of Xinyang teahouses keeps unknown, it is widely accepted that they emerged within urban Xinyang during the Ming Dynasty. In the Qing Dynasty, teahouses, with different couplets on tea and tea culture, could be found everywhere in Xinyang. Nowadays, with modern development, there is a wide variety of tea cafes, teahouses, and tea restaurants in Xinyang. On the "tea culture street" situated along the Shi River in Xinyang, there are over thirty teahouses and tea art houses that attract large numbers of tourists and most importantly tea drinkers every day.

(2) Tea Art Performance

Tea art performance, also known as the Tea Dao performance, is an art that

采茶姑娘茶艺表演（信阳学院冯春晓摄影）
Tea Picking Girl and Tea Art Performance (Photography by Feng Chunxiao, Xinyang University)

　　信阳茶艺表演由茶艺师、司茶女、主持人组成，一般为8～10人，表演一个小时左右。茶艺表演所用器具包括：茶船、茶具、茶海（也称为茶盅）、闻香杯、品茗杯、随手泡、茶罐、赏茶盘、茶巾、茶则、茶筷、茶漏、茶匙、茶针等。

　　信阳茶艺表演环节分为十道程序。第一道：鉴赏佳茗。茶艺师从茶罐里取出信阳毛尖干茶置于赏茶盘中，请评委及来宾观赏干茶。第二道：提取清泉。茶艺师净手提水。第三道：清洁茶具。茶艺师将随手泡的泉水注入玻璃茶壶内，依次倒入闻香杯、品茗杯，再用茶筷夹洗茶杯，清洁茶具。第四道：佳人入宫。茶艺师先用茶则从茶盒中取出信阳毛尖，再用茶匙轻轻拨入壶内。第五道：涤尽凡尘。茶艺师把注入茶壶的第一道茶水倒掉，俗称"洗茶"。第六道：湿润泡茶。茶艺师提壶采用"回旋注水法"向壶中注水少许，浸润茶芽。第七道：有凤来仪。茶艺师提

perfectly combines tea with culture. Xinyang tea performance adopts features from other tea art performances and also develops many of its own. These performances display the uniqueness of the tea leaves: thin with pointy edges, and the tea flavor: rich and refreshing, as well as the long history of Xinyang tea. Today, shows are not only performed locally to support economic growth, but also are brought to metropolitan cities such as Beijing, Shanghai, Zhengzhou, Wuhan, etc., showing Xinyang tea culture on various stages and occasions and receiving applause from audiences of all parts of China.

Xinyang tea art performances take usually about an hour and consist of eight to ten performers, including tea art specialists, tea servers, and hosts. Wares used in the performance include: tea plate, tea set, tea pitcher, aroma cup, "pinming" cup (used for observing the tea leaves), kettle, tea canister, tea tray, towel, dry tea holder, tea tongs, tea strainer, tea spoon and tea needle, etc.

There are ten steps in the Xinyang tea art performance. The first step: Tea Sighting. Tea art specialists place the Maojian from the tea canister onto the plate where professional judges comment on the quality of the dry tea. The second step: Spring Water Extraction. Tea art specialists fetch the spring water after cleaning their hands. The third step: Tea Set Cleansing. Tea art specialists pour the spring water into the glass tea kettle, aroma cup, "pinming" cup accordingly, and clean the tea set with tea tongs. The fourth step: Inviting the "Beauty." Tea art specialists take the Maojian tea out of the tea canister with a caddy spoon and then dip the tea into the kettle with a teaspoon. The fifth step: Tea Cleansing, also known as Tea Rinsing. The liquid, used to clean the tea, is being removed from the tea kettle at this time. The sixth step: Gentle Brewing. A little water is poured into the kettle, soaking the tea buds into water. The seventh step : The "Phoenix" Paying Respects. Tea art specialists pour out the tea from the kettle, moving the kettle away and towards another kettle while pouring. This movement is repeated three times and is called "phoenix nodding thrice". After pouring, bubbles on top of the tea are removed with the kettle cap, known as "spring's greeting". The eighth step: Tea Back into the Tea Pitcher. Tea art specialists pour the tea into the tea pitcher, separating the leaves and liquid, creating an even taste. The ninth step: Distribution. Tea art specialists fill up 70% of aroma cups with tea liquor, leaving 30% of the cup blank. The tenth step: Serving. The Maojian tea is finally served by

壶倒茶，上下提拉注水，反复三次，雅称"凤凰三点头"，然后用壶盖轻轻拂去茶汤表面泡沫，雅称"春风拂面"。第八道：玉液回海。茶艺师将壶中茶水倒入茶海，使茶汤分离，浓淡均匀。第九道：平分秋色。茶艺师将茶盅之水依次斟入闻香杯（斟茶七分满，留下三分是情义）。第十道：敬奉宾客。茶艺师双手捧起茶杯，依次向宾客敬茶，请宾客品茗。

信阳茶艺表演（信阳学院冯春晓摄影）
Xinyang Tea Art Performance (Photography by Feng Chunxiao, Xinyang University)

宾客品茶时，采用"三龙护鼎"式端杯手法，先观汤色之匀雅，碧绿明亮，后品滋味之韵喉，分三口品茗。第一口，先润唇，柔软含香；第二口，再润舌，鲜醇清香；第三口，后润喉，回喉甘甜。

（3）信阳茶文化节

创办于1992年，已连续成功举办28届的信阳茶文化节，始终坚持"发展、合作、健康、和谐"的办节理念，以"弘扬茶文化，发展茶产业，促进茶流通"为出发点，以服务茶企、茶商、茶界为切入点，取得了巨大的社会效益和经济效益。多年来，信阳市紧跟时代发展，不断创新办节形式，先后推出"茶＋节会""茶＋旅游""茶＋饮食""茶＋

the tea art specialists, with both hands holding the cup, for the audiences to enjoy.

When enjoying the tea, drinkers should hold the tea cups with their thumb and index finger while placing the middle finger at the cup's bottom and curve their last two fingers. Drinkers are expected to first observe the tea liquor before drinking and finish a cup of tea in three sips. In the first sip, the tea moisturizes the lips and leaves the tea aroma on it. During the second sip, the drinkers moisturize their tongue and taste the freshness. After the third sip, the tea may soothe the throat and leave a rich aftertaste.

品茗香茶（信阳学院冯春晓摄影）
Tea Drinking（Photography by Feng Chunxiao, Xinyang University)

(3) Xinyang Tea Culture Festival

Initiated in 1992, there have been twenty-eight Xinyang Tea Culture Festivals in total. The festivals consistently uphold the concept of "development, collaboration, health, and peace" with the purpose of spreading tea culture, promoting the circulation of tea trade and serving for the tea enterprises, tea traders and tea industries. And the holding of the festivals has actually brought about great social and economic benefits to the city. Over the years, Xinyang, keeping pace with the times, constantly innovated the forms of the festival, including a combination of tea with festivals, tea with travelling, tea with gourmet food, tea with ecology, and tea with poverty-alleviation issues, etc. Activities such

生态""茶+脱贫"等节会主题,通过举办信阳毛尖传统手工炒制大赛、环南湾湖特色茶旅体验活动、信阳茶歌茶舞汇报演出、国际茶文化与茶产业发展研讨会等,使信阳茶文化节的专业性、开放性、国际性、市场性不断提升,逐渐成长为具有豫南风情和中原特色的茶专业节会、中国茶界一个重要的节会品牌,为茶界交流合作提供了高端平台。2018年5月,信阳茶文化节荣获"中国茶事样板十佳"第二名。

信阳茶文化节极大带动了信阳茶叶的出口增长。截至目前,信阳市全市共有茶叶出口备案企业21家。2019年,信阳市共出口茶叶6519.7吨,占同期全省出口量的83.6%;出口总值1.43亿元,占同期全省出口值的28.5%。主要出口茶叶品种为绿茶,少量红茶,主要出口阿尔及利亚、尼日利亚、摩洛哥、乌兹别克斯坦、阿富汗、蒙古、韩国、加拿大和中国香港等国家和地区,所出口的茶叶档次和均价有所提高。

信阳名片:看红看绿看蓝天 品山品水品毛尖(信阳学院冯春晓摄影)
Red Culture, Blue Sky, Crystal Clear Water and Xinyang Maojian Tea(Photography by Feng Chunxiao, Xinyang University)

信阳茶文化节也充分带动了信阳茶文化旅游的兴起和繁荣。近年来,信阳把茶文化旅游项目纳入《信阳市旅游总体规划》,以信阳茶文化节为载体,依托丰富的茶文化旅游资源,积极探索、创新发展,先后规划

as Xinyang Maojian Traditional Manual Tea Stir-frying Contest, Round-the-Nanwan-Lake Tea Culture Experiencing Tour, Xinyang Tea Songs and Dances Performances, and International Tea Culture and Tea Industry Development Seminar were held in the festivals, which all made the festivals more professional, open, international, and marketable. Tea festivals also became an important part of the local culture, an irreplaceable ritual in Chinese tea, and a platform of communication for tea lovers. In May 2018, Xinyang Tea Culture Festival ranked second in the "Top Ten Tea Culture Events in China".

Xinyang Tea Culture Festival has greatly brought about the growth of Xinyang tea export. Up to now, there are a total of 21 tea exporting companies in Xinyang. In 2019, the total amount of tea export amounted to 6,519.7 tons, 83.6% of the Henan Province tea export. The total value of tea export added up to 0.143 billion *yuan*, 28.5% of the gross tea export value in Henan Province. The tea, mainly green tea with some black tea, is exported with better quality at higher price to Algeria, Nigeria, Morocco, Uzbekistan, Afghanistan, Mongolia, South Korea, Canada, and Chinese Hong Kong.

Xinyang Tea Culture Festival also fully brought about the development and boom of the local tea culture tourism. Recently, tea culture tourism has been integrated into the city's overall tourism plan by the Xinyang municipal government. With Xinyang tea as the core, many culture projects were built for tourism, including the Nanwan Lake Tea Island, Wenxin Tea Culture Garden, Guangyi Tea Culture Garden, Guangshan Tea Set Museum, etc. In addition to these major projects, there are hundreds of tea-tourism establishments in Xinyang City, including more than 100 scaled tea culture tourism locations, 85 tea gardens, 350 tea farm hotels, and more than 800 recreational tea farms, thus initially forming a number of unique travelling routes. Tea culture tourism, together with red culture tourism and tea village environmental tourism, becomes the striking feature and highlight of Xinyang tourism promotion. The image of "red culture, blue sky, crystal clear water together with Xinyang Maojian" has become the beautiful card of Xinyang all-around tourism.

Tea, as a bright city card of Xinyang, bears her history and her promising future. The Xinyang Tea Culture Festival has witnessed and is promoting the change of people's view and the change of both urban and rural development.

了南湾湖茶岛、文新茶文化园、广义茶文化园、光山茶具博物馆等一批大型茶文化旅游园区。全市成规模茶文化休闲旅游处所 100 余家，旅游观赏茶园 85 处；农家茶园小酒店 350 个，亦茶亦旅、茶旅结合的农户达到 800 余户：初步形成了多条特色茶风情旅游线路。茶文化旅游与红色文化游、绿色茶乡游相辅相成、相得益彰，成为对外旅游推广的特色和亮点。"看红看绿看蓝天、品山品水品毛尖"已成为信阳全域旅游一张靓丽的名片。

茶，传承着信阳的历史，成就了信阳的名片，承载着信阳的希望。信阳茶文化节见证和推动着信阳的观念之变、城市之变、茶乡之变、发展之变。

信阳茶文化旅游(信阳学院冯葆炜摄影)
Tea and the Tea Culture Tourism in Xinyang (Photography by Feng Baowei, Xinyang University)

二、信阳菜：豫楚风味

在林林总总的烹饪大家庭里，作为河南省地方菜，信阳菜过去可谓是"养在深闺人未识"。然而，随着近年来的发展，信阳菜终于继鸡公山、南湾湖、信阳毛尖之后，逐渐向世人崭露出她"天生丽质难自弃"的风采，成为信阳的又一个品牌。

1. 信阳菜内涵

信阳菜，从狭义上讲，是地理意义上的信阳菜；从宏观上讲，她是个立体、综合的概念，包括物质层面上的信阳菜、文化层面上的信阳菜和技术层面上的信阳菜。

首先，物质层面上的信阳菜，包括信阳茶、信阳水、信阳菜（烹饪原料），这是构成信阳菜的基础与前提。信阳人之所以称为信阳人，与他们饮茶、吃米、擅烹鱼类是相提并论的，而这些又都与信阳人具体的生存环境密不可分。

其次，文化层面上的信阳菜，包括饮食心理、饮食习俗、饮食传说以及浸润其每一个细节的主流文化传统。约从春秋战国时期开始，信阳长期属于楚文化的范畴，不仅深深地打上了楚文化的烙印，而且揭开了信阳饮食文化的新篇章。于是，信阳菜与楚菜大体一致，喜欢食羹（汤）、合烧（数种肉拼合在一起）、野味以及腌腊等冷膳制作。信阳菜承继楚菜的优良传统，历经沧桑，与时俱进，最终形成了目前独具特色的菜肴风格。

最后，技术层面上的信阳菜，包括技术人才及其影响、多种技法的交叉运用。信阳菜的技术人才包括御厨传人、豫菜正宗传人和擅烹地方菜的信阳人，还包括把粤菜和川菜与信阳地方菜科学结合起来的广东人和四川人，以及借鉴鄂菜技法的年轻信阳人。这些信阳餐饮界的精英，在信阳原料这个前提下，八仙过海，各显神通，或一人多能，或多种技

II. Xinyang Cuisine: A Blending of the Flavors Both of Henan and Hubei Cuisines

Among various cuisines in China, Xinyang cuisine, one kind of the local cuisines in Henan Province, is not famous, just as the pretty lady is not well-known due to growing up in her boudoir. However, with the local development in recent years, Xinyang cuisine, like a charming lady, gradually reveals its unique flavor, and becomes another new brand in Xinyang, along with the Rooster Mountain, Nanwan Lake, and Xinyang Maojian tea.

1. The Connotation of Xinyang Cuisine

Xinyang cuisine, in a narrow sense, is Xinyang dishes in the geographical sense; while in the macro level, it is a three-dimensional and comprehensive concept, including Xinyang cuisine on the material level, Xinyang cuisine on the cultural level and Xinyang cuisine on the technical level.

First of all, Xinyang cuisine on the material level includes Xinyang Maojian tea, Xinyang water and different ingredients used in dishes, which make up of the basis of the Xinyang cuisine. It caters to the habit of tea drinking, rice eating and fish cooking of local Xinyang people, which is closely related to the specific living environment of Xinyang people.

Secondly, Xinyang cuisine on the cultural level includes diet psychology, diet custom, diet legend and those mainstream cultural traditions penetrating into the diet habit. Started as early in the Spring and Autumn and the Warring States periods, Xinyang was the territory of the Chu State, and as a result, was greatly influenced by the culture in Chu State and since then it opened a new chapter for Xinyang diet culture. Xinyang cuisine is very similar to that of Chu State, favoring porridges, meat pots, wild animals, and those cold dishes like cured food. Xinyang cuisine maintains much diet tradition in Chu State, but at the same time develops based on the traditional cuisine in Chu State, forming the unique Xinyang cuisine.

Last but not least, Xinyang cuisine on the technical level includes those gifted chefs and the combination and blending of all kinds of cooking techniques. There assemble chefs like the successors of royal cuisine, the successors of Henan cuisine,

法交织运用，互相借鉴又相互融合，极大地丰富了信阳的餐饮市场，适应了人们多变的消费心理，从而形成信阳菜烹饪体系，提升了信阳菜整体的烹制水平。

2. 信阳菜分类

传统上把菜谱菜肴分为宫廷菜、官府菜、酒肆菜、寺庵菜及民间菜。长期以来，信阳没有居于国家的政治、经济、文化中心，虽有御厨传人，但宫廷菜一直对信阳影响不大。鉴于信阳菜定型较晚，编者根据其自身特性，从消费终端和烹制特点两方面入手，暂把信阳菜分为炖菜、乡土菜、筵席菜、卤腊凉菜及风味小吃五大类。其中，最能代表信阳菜独特魅力的是炖菜。可以毫不夸张地说，在信阳菜的谱系里，到处都能看到"炖菜"的影子，几乎到了无菜不炖、无炖不成筵席的地步。

从信阳菜的原料构成来看，可分为三大类、三小类。

第一大类是水产类。信阳作为河南的"小江南"，水产养殖十分发达，水产品十分丰富。仅南湾水库，就盛产花鲢、白鲢、鲤鱼、鲫鱼、鳊鱼、鲂鱼、鳜鱼、鲶鱼、银鱼、黄颡鱼、乌鱼、黄鳝、甲鱼、青虾、河鳖等多种野生水产品。据统计，信阳可食鱼类有100种，虾贝类近50种，其中南湾鱼、光山青虾远近闻名。

闻名遐迩的南湾生态鱼头汤
The Well-known Nanwan Fishhead Soup

the local people who are skilled in Xinyang cuisine, Cantonese and Sichuan people who combine their local cuisine with Xinyang cuisine, and Xinyang youngsters who often draw inspiration from Hubei cuisine. They take advantage of local food material with different kinds of cooking techniques, which leads to the development of catering industry in Xinyang. The unique cooking style of Xinyang cuisine comes into being to adapt for different customer demands, which, in turns, stimulates the cooking of Xinyang cuisine to a whole new level.

2. Types of Xinyang Cuisine

Ancient Chinese cuisines are classified as royal dishes, Guanfu/governmental dishes, restaurant dishes, temple/nunnery dishes, and folk dishes. Since Xinyang has never been the political or economic center of the nation, royal cuisine has little impact on Xinyang cuisine, even though there are successors of royal cuisine in Xinyang. Since Xinyang cuisine was formed at a relatively later time, the Xinyang cuisine has been divided into five categories based on the consumers and cooking techniques, namely stewed dish, local dish, festival dish, pickled dish or cured meat , and appetizers and snacks. Stewed dishes are the best representation of Xinyang cuisine because they can be found on every table in Xinyang and there is also a local saying going that "you can't have a meal without stews".

According to the ingredients, Xinyang food could be classified into three major types and three minor classes.

Aquatic products are one of the three majors. Xinyang is called the "Jiangnan of Henan" for its thriving fishery industry and diverse aquatic products. There is a great variety of aquatic products in the Nanwan Lake, including spotted silver carp, silver carp, common carp, crucian carp, Parabramis Pekinensis, gurnard, mandarin fish, catfish, icefish, Pelteobagrus fulvidraco, black mullet, ricefield eels, soft-shelled turtle, freshwater shrimps, and river soft-shelled turtle, etc. Statistics show that there are 100 types of edible fish and nearly 50 kinds of shrimps and shellfish in Xinyang, of which the most famous ones are the Nanwan fish and Guangshan freshwater shrimps.

The second major type is livestock and poultry, which mainly includes Huainan pig, Huai goat, Gushi chicken, Guangshan goose, Huainan shelduck, Sanhuang chicken, and Huaying duck, upon which series of livestock and poultry

第二大类是畜禽类，主要有淮南猪、槐山羊、固始鸡、光山鹅、淮南麻鸭、三黄鸡、华英鸭，从而形成固始鸡系列、固始皮丝系列、华英鸭系列、蛋制品系列。它们基本构成了信阳菜的主体菜肴和核心菜肴。

第三大类是素菜类，如南部山区的野生食用菌、山野菜；北部尤其是沿史、灌、淮河流域生产的四时蔬菜，基本上无污染、无公害，营养成分齐全，开发潜力较大。

三小类是指：

第一小类是蛋制品类：举凡鸡、鸭、鹅、鹌鹑蛋，应有尽有，可炒，可炸，可煎，可炖，可蒸，可卤，可腌，可制作蛋粉、松花蛋。

第二小类是豆制品类：信阳干豆腐、水豆腐，因原料、水质及制作工艺上的特点，质量在全国均为上乘。至于豆芽、豆脑、罗山千张、潢川二簿、董家河豆筋、苏仙石鸭蛋干、商城豆腐渣均是质佳味美，可以加工制成上百个品种。

第三小类是咸腊菜类：酸甜咸辣，风味多样，不论是筵席点缀，还是家常享用，都有一定的消费群体。如咸鸭蛋、咸鸡蛋、酸豆角、箭杆白、咸腊菜（雪里蕻），至今魅力不减。

3. 信阳菜特点

从口味上来看，信阳菜以咸、烂、香、微辣、醇厚、味浓、色微重、爽滑为主味。从地域上看，主要是受湖北、河南、安徽的影响所致。与川菜相比较，信阳菜微辣而不麻，似香辣范畴；与湘菜的腊味相比，咸香而不含烟熏；与鄂菜相比，胡椒的用量轻于武汉；与徽菜相比，芡汁稍小；与豫菜相比，口味稍嫌偏重、偏辣。

从烹饪技法上看，民间烹饪方法以炒、焖为主，炖煮次之，还有蒸、煎、炸、溜、汆、卤等方法，在原料保管上采用了腌、腊、风干等方法。比如腌制的蔬菜有雪里蕻、箭杆白、豇豆等，鲜香可口，刺激食欲，是佐酒助兴的风味食品。在烹饪技法上，"炖"法占有突出的地位，主要

are manufactured, such as the Gushi chicken series, Gushi pork skin slice series, Huaying duck series, and egg products series, etc. They make up the majority of Xinyang cuisine.

The third major type is vegetables, consisting of wild edible mushrooms and wild vegetables in the southern mountainous areas and vegetables available for four seasons along the Shihe River, Guanhe River, and Huaihe River Basin to the north. They are largely pollution-free, rich in nutrition and production potential.

The three minor types:

The first minor type is egg products, including henapple, ducks' egg, geese' egg, and quails' egg, etc. They can be cooked in such different ways as sauteing, frying, stewing, steaming, pot-stewing, and pickling. In addition, they can be made into egg powder or preserved into century eggs.

The second is soy products: Xinyang dried tofu (beancurd) and soft tofu are superior in quality due to its ingredients, good quality of water and production process. Other soy products, amounting to over a hundred, including bean sprouts, tofu pudding, Luoshan dried tofu sheets, Dongjiahe beancurd, Suxianshi dried duck eggs, and Shangcheng tofu dregs, are also delicious and tasteful.

李家寨豆腐（信阳学院冯春晓摄影）
Lijiazhai Tofu (Photography by Feng Chunxiao, Xinyang University)

The last minor is salt cured food with various flavors such as sour, sweet, salty,

以信阳闷罐肉、潢川甲鱼泡馍、固始炖鸡、商城家常风味炖菜为代表。2021年，商城炖菜烹饪技艺被列入第五批河南省非物质文化遗产代表性项目保护单位名单。

信阳闷罐肉（信阳学院冯春晓摄影）
Xinyang Pot Stewed Pork (Photography by Feng Chunxiao, Xinyang University)

商城老鸭汤
Shangcheng Duck Soup

从原料来源来看，信阳菜倡导绿色食品，大量使用野生原料。信阳是全国污染较小的无公害生态农业示范区，拥有丰富的野生、绿色动植物资源。如食用菌有香菇、黑木耳、竹荪等；药食两用植物有信阳灵芝、桔梗、商茯苓、天麻、野山楂、八角莲；蔬菜瓜果类有信阳黄心菜、商

and spicy. These dishes can be found everywhere from formal festival dinners to casual home meals. Salty duck eggs, salty eggs, pickled green beans, pickled Jian' ganbai (one type of Chinese cabbages), and preserved potherb mustard are the most popular and common dishes of the salt cured food.

3. Characteristics of Xinyang Cuisine

In terms of flavor, Xinyang cuisine is noted for salty, soft, smooth, aromatic and mildly spicy in taste and lightly heavier in color. When taking geographical factor into consideration, Xinyang cuisine is largely influenced by those in Hubei, Henan and Anhui provinces. Unlike Chuan cuisine (cuisine of Sichuan Province), which is famous for its hot and spicy, Xinyang cuisine is mildly spicy and aromatic. Compared with Hunan cuisine, Xinyang salt cured food tastes salty and savory but not fumigating. Xinyang cuisine uses less pepper than Hubei cuisine, less soup than Anhui cuisine, and is spicier than Henan cuisine.

In terms of cooking methods, Xinyang cuisine is mostly sauteed or braised, sometimes stewed or boiled. There are also ways like steaming, pan frying, deep fried, sauteed, quick-boiled or pot-stewed. The ways like pickling, curing and air drying would also be used to store the ingredients of food. Common salt cured and pickled dishes are preserved potherb mustard, Jian'ganbai (either pickled green leaves vegetable or black-eyed pea), having rich flavor and stimulating appetite. The stewing method plays a vital role in Xinyang food. The famous stewing dishes are Xinyang pot stewed pork, Huangchuan foam bun with stewed softshell turtle, Gushi stewed chicken, and stewed dishes with Shangcheng flavor. In 2021, the stewing technique with Shangcheng flavor was enlisted in the fifth batch of Representative Items of Intangible Cultural Heritage in Henan Province.

When it comes to food material, Xinyang cuisine advocates using natural food material under the programme of green food. Xinyang, the eco-agricultural demonstration area in China, has natural resources for wild animals and wild plants. As to wild plants, edible mushrooms include shiitake, wood ears, and bamboo mushrooms. Wild plants for both diet and medical use include Xinyang ganoderma, Platycodon grandiflorum, Shangcheng tuckahoe, Rhizoma Gastrodiae, wild hawthorn, and Dysosma versipellis. There are also

城黄花菜、潢川州姜、固始萝卜、罗山箭杆白、固始雪里蕻、新县山野菜、信阳拳菜等；还有板栗、银杏果、南湾鱼、固始鸡、信阳百蛋鹅、商城麻鸭等原料。其品种之多，数量之众，质量之优，都是其他地方菜系所不能比拟的。

fruits and vegetables such as Xinyang yellow heart cabbage, Shangcheng daylily, Huangchuan ginger, Gushi radish, Luoshan Jian' ganbai, Gushi preserved potherb mustard, Xinxian wild vegetable, and Xinyang fiddlehead. Other types of wildlife such as chestnuts, ginkgo nuts, Nanwan fish, Gushi chicken, Xinyang goose, and Shangcheng shelduck could also be found. To sum up, the wild food material in Xinyang is numerous in variety, large in quantity and high in quality, which makes Xinyang cuisine incomparable to other local cuisine in China.

第五章

民俗篇：淮河民俗文化

Chapter 5

Folk Customs: Folk Cultures Along the Huaihe River

民俗又称民间文化，是指一个民族或一个社会群体在长期的生产实践和社会生活中逐渐形成并世代相传、较为稳定的文化事项，简单地说就是民间流行的风尚、习俗，即民众的生活、生产中约定俗成的一些习惯和应遵守的某种规范。

淮河流域的民俗可以分为物质生活民俗、社会生活民俗和精神生活民俗三大类。

一、物质生活民俗

物质生活民俗是指生产民俗、工商业民俗和生活民俗，主要指农业、渔业、养殖等物质资料生产方面的民俗，和手工业、服务业等物质资料加工方面的民俗，以及衣、食、住、行等物质消费方面的民俗。

1. 生产民俗

生产民俗主要指农业、渔业、养殖等物质资料生产方面的民俗。

（1）水稻种植民俗

淮河流域是中国最早的稻作文化区，豫南地区气候温和湿润，水系发达，得天独厚的自然条件使该地区种稻子的生产习俗传承至今，并逐渐形成信阳大米的品牌。

在息县，传统种植的一种稻谷有个非常好听的名字——香稻丸。

香稻丸仅产于息县的夏庄、项店一带，是河南名产。其色青白，粒粒饱满似珍珠，有异香，素有"一块稻香满坡，一撮米香满锅，一家做饭香四邻，一盅香酒香满桌"的盛称。明清两代，香稻丸皆为贡品。

用香稻丸、粳米、莲米加红枣熬成的"三米汤"，是极好的滋补品，具有滋阴、降火、生津、健脾、养胃等功效。息县以香稻丸为原料制成的香米贡酒，便是"一盅香酒香满桌"，味道醇厚，芳香可口。2021年，香稻丸种植加工技艺被列入第五批河南省非物质文化遗产代表性项目保

Folk customs, or folk cultures, refer to the relatively stable cultural matters which are gradually formed and passed down from generation to generation in a nation or a society during the long-term labor practice and social life. Briefly speaking, it is the popular fashion or customs among people, i.e., the habits which are conventionalized and regulations that people should abide by in the life and work.

民俗文化传统戏《顶椅》(信阳学院冯葆炜摄影)
Heading a Chair, Traditional Folk Culture Opera (Photography by Feng Baowei, Xinyang University)

The folk customs along the Huaihe River Basin can be classified into three branches: customs on material life, social life and spiritual life.

I. Folk Customs on Material Life

The folk customs on material life include those of agriculture, industry, commerce, and everyday life, such as the ways of cultivation, fishing, farming, etc., the customs in the handicraft industry, service industry, etc. and the customs about consumption of daily necessities.

1. Folk Customs on Material Production

The folk customs on material production mainly refer to those on the

护单位名单。

息县香稻丸
Xixian Fragrant Rice

（2）渔业民俗

南湾鱼盛产于有"中原第一湖"美誉的信阳南湾湖，独特的气候条件和优质的水资源赋予了南湾鱼肉质细嫩、鲜美爽口的特性，年产量达180万公斤，是地道的无公害绿色食品。尤其南湾花鲢，经农业部食品检测机构测定，含有蛋白质、脂肪、人体必需的多种维生素及稀有元素，

《捕鱼时节》：绿色天然无污染的南湾鱼（吴晓军摄影）
The Fishing Season: The Nanwan Fish, Green Food Without Pollution (Photography by Wu Xiaojun)

production of goods and materials such as agriculture, fishery and poultry breeding.

(1) Folk Customs on Rice Cultivation

The Huaihe River Basin is the earliest rice-growing area in China. The climate in southern Henan is mild and humid and the water system is developed. Such natural conditions make the custom of rice-growing in this area gradually forge the identity of Xinyang rice.

In Xixian County, a kind of rice traditionally cultivated has a very pleasant name—fragrant rice.

Fragrant rice is one of the special local products in Henan Province, only planted in the areas of Xiazhuang and Xiangdian villages. It is bluish white and each grain looks like a plump pearl. This rice has unique scent, which enjoys such a good reputation: the scent of ripe rice spreads on the hillside; the scent of steaming rice suffuses in the pot; the scent of the food pervades in the neighborhood; the scent of rice wine floats on the dining table. In the Ming and Qing dynasties, this kind of rice was the tribute to the emperors.

The Three-Rice Soup, a kind of wonderful nutriment, is made of fragrant rice, polished round-grained rice, lotus seeds, and dates. It has the functions of nourishing Yin to cool the blood, promoting the secretion of saliva, and strengthening the spleen and stomach. In Xixian County, the rice wine made of fragrant rice is fragrant and mellow, inspiring the famous quote "the scent of rice wine floating on the dining table". In 2021, the planting and processing technology of fragrant rice was listed as the representative project in the 5th batch of Henan Intangible Cultural Heritage.

(2) Folk Customs on Fishery

The Nanwan fish is abundant in the Nanwan Lake which is known as "the first lake in Central China". Due to the remarkable climate and high-quality water resources, the Nanwan fish is delicious, tasting tender and refreshing. It is an unadulterated green food with an annual output of 1,800,000 kilos. According to the testing from relevant food safety and inspection department in China, spotted silver carp, one type of well-known Nanwan fish, contains protein, fat, various vitamins essential for the human body, and rare elements, among which selenium, an anti-cancer element, is three times more than that in common fish.

其中有抗癌元素之称的"硒"含量是普通鱼类的 3 倍以上。

南湾鱼整个养殖水面有 7.1 万亩,从不喂任何人工饲料,每年 11 月份开始投放鱼苗,经过至少两年野生状态下的生长,达不到 2.5 千克以上的规格,或不到大规模捕捞的季节,鱼儿就暂时囤养网箱里。南湾湖还通过了无公害水产品生产基地认证。

(3)养殖业民俗

淮河流域一直都有养鸭、养鹅的传统,华英鸭和皖西、固始白鹅是其中的代表。

皖西、固始白鹅,是经过劳动人民长期人工选育和自然驯化而形成的优良地方品种。鹅苗经过 3～4 个月的放牧,体重已接近成年鹅,但很少宰杀,继续饲养到 11 月,至农历"小雪"前后,在宰前 20 天将鹅圈养,限制其活动,以稻谷等饲料进行催肥,称为"栈鹅"。制作的"烤鹅"和"腊鹅",鲜嫩可口,风味独特,"固始鹅块"更是一绝。皖西、固始白鹅产毛量高,羽绒洁白,弹性好,蓬松质佳,尤其以绒毛的绒朵大而著称。产区每年出口羽绒占全国出口量的 10%,居全国第一位。鹅皮可鞣制裘皮,柔软蓬松,保暖性好。

固始白鹅(信阳学院冯春晓摄影)

The Gushi White Goose (Photography by Feng Chunxiao, Xinyang University)

The total area for breeding Nanwan fish reaches up to about 4,733 hectares. A large number of fish fry are released into the Nanwan Lake each November and grow up for at least 2 years in a natural environment without any artificial feed. They would be kept temporarily in the net cage waiting for sale when less than 2.5 kilos or before the season for mass fishing. The Nanwan Lake is also certified as a pollution-free aquatic production base.

鱼鹰捕鱼——传统捕鱼活化石（信阳学院冯春晓摄影）
Osprey Fishing—A Living Fossil of Traditional Fishing Artistry (Photography by Feng Chunxiao, Xinyang University)

(3) Folk Customs on Poultry Breeding

There has always been a tradition of breeding ducks and geese in the Huaihe River Basin, among which Huaying ducks, Wanxi (western Anhui Province) and Gushi white geese are the most famous.

The Wanxi and Gushi white geese are the excellent local varieties formed through long-term artificial breeding and natural domestication. In three to four months, the goslings have grown up, but few are killed or sold until the lunar "Slight Snow" term in November. In the three weeks before the geese are killed, they are kept in cages to restrict their movement and are fattened with food such as rice. This is known as "storing goose". The "roasted goose" and "cured goose"

2. 工商业民俗

信阳是民俗之乡、传统手工技艺之乡。这里主要介绍一种手工业民俗——毛布底鞋的制作。

商城县、新县的毛布底鞋，是一种纯手工、纯棉布的千层底鞋，工艺复杂，工序繁缛，每一双鞋都需经过8道大工序，62道小工序才能完成。最重要、最耗时的工序是纳千层底，素有"棉布填千层，麻线扎千针"的说法。

商城纯棉布千层底鞋制作工艺（信阳学院冯春晓摄影）
Cotton Shoes with Multi-layer Soles Made in Shangcheng County（Photography by Feng Chunxiao, Xinyang University）

商城毛布底鞋的制作过程中，还有一个工艺非常独特，叫反绱鞋。就是反着将鞋面上在鞋底上，然后再将其翻过来，这样的方法使上鞋的针脚藏在鞋子里面，使鞋子更美观。这个步骤需要力气大的男工来完成。绿色、环保、健康、传统，成就了信阳毛布底鞋手工制作技艺的传承，目前已成为当地的支柱产业。

are fresh, tender and delicious with a unique flavor, and the "Gushi goose" is a must eat for gourmands. Goose feathers from Wanxi and Gushi geese are white, soft and fluffy. The annual output of goose feather accounts for 10% of the total exports of the Country, ranking first in China. Goose skin can be made into fur coats, or bedding.

2. Folk Customs in Industry and Commerce

Xinyang is the home of unique local folk culture and traditional handicrafts. Here we will introduce one handicraft folk custom—the production process of shoes with cotton cloth soles.

This kind of shoes made in Shangcheng and Xinxian counties are pure handmade shoes with multi-layer soles. Each pair of shoes is made elaborately with 8 large-scale processes and 62 small-scale processes, during which sewing multi-layer soles is the most important and time-consuming process, as a popular saying claims "the soles made of multi-layer cotton cloth need as many as thousands of stitches".

商城三多堂制作出的各种传统布鞋（信阳学院冯春晓摄影）
Traditional Cotton Shoes Made in Sanduotang, Shangcheng County (Photography by Feng Chunxiao, Xinyang University)

3. 生活民俗

生活民俗主要指人们衣、食、住、行等物质消费方面的风俗习惯。因饮食方面前面已涉及，这里不再赘述。

（1）衣

新中国成立前，中国人贫富差距较大，有富人和穷人之分。那时候的包括淮河流域的穿衣习俗是，富家的男性穿长衫和长袍，下身穿裤子，质地多为棉、丝绸或皮毛；脚穿尖口布鞋。穷家男性穿短袄、短衫，冬天短袄大棉裤束腰带御寒，质地为家织粗布；一般穿草鞋，雨天光脚，雪天穿木屐。富家年轻女性穿宽袖短衣，袖口有三道颜色各不相同的镶边，称为"兰香"，下身穿到脚踝的长裙，质地一般为绸缎；脚穿绣花鞋。中老年女性穿大襟过膝袍、褂，下穿罗裙。穷家女性穿家织布质地的短袄、短衫，由于穿裙子不便参加劳动，故以穿裤子为主，服装颜色以大红大绿为特征，有"红四十（岁），绿到老"之说。

新中国成立初期，各行各业穿蓝色、灰色干部服（男女同款式）的增多，甚至老年男女也以穿干部服为荣。改革开放以来，衣着款式翻新，男女青年穿红着绿，花样翻新，颜色各异。可以说，时尚是现在信阳服饰的代名词。

（2）住

信阳人在住的方面有自己的风俗，尤其对起房盖屋极其重视，是居家一大盛事，亲朋、好友、邻里须来相帮并致恭贺礼。

由于各县区风俗不同，豫南建房的讲究概括为"武脊六兽"。房屋的屋脊用陶雕覆盖，陶雕是用陶土做成的动物模型烧制而成，虎、狮、龙、鹿、羊等陶雕压在屋脊上，称为"武脊"。正门门头上方也雕以虎、狮之类猛兽。两厢房屋脊雕以鱼或鸽、鹤。屋脊雕兽证明主人富有，象征平安、吉祥、如意、长寿。经济条件差的小户人家用"文脊"，就是不加装饰的脊瓦或胶泥覆顶，也叫"泥鳅脊"。

When making the shoes in Shangcheng County, a unique technique called "anti-phase sole-stitching" is adopted, that is, sewing the vamp on the soles firstly, then turning it inside out. In this way, the stitches are hidden inside the shoes, making them look more beautiful. However, this step requires a strong man to complete. Healthy, traditional and environment-friendly, this handicraft has been passed on and remains a mainstay in the local economy.

3. Folk Customs on Daily Life

Daily life folk customs mainly refer to the customs and habits of material consumption such as clothing, food, housing and transportation. Since the diet has been discussed in the previous chapter, it is not included here.

(1) Clothing

Before the founding of the People's Republic of China (PRC), there was a large gap between the rich and the poor. The dress custom at that time along the Huaihe River was that the rich men wore a long gown and a long robe with trousers mostly made of cotton, silk or fur, and pointed cotton shoes. Poor men wore only short *mian'ao* (cotton-padded coat) and cotton jacket. In winter they wore the short *mian'ao* and loose *mian'ku* (cotton-padded trousers) made of homespun cloth, usually with a belt to keep out the coldness. They usually wore clogs in winter and straw sandals in other seasons, even bare feet in rainy days. The rich young women wore short clothes with wide sleeves and three different colored bands on the cuffs, called "Lan Xiang" (literally the fragrance of the orchid), with ankle-length skirt, usually made of silk, and embroidered shoes. Middle-aged and elderly women wore knee-length gowns (a Chinese-style garment with buttons on the right) and silk skirts. The poor women, similar to the men, wore only short homespun *mian'ao* and cotton jacket. Since it was inconvenient to wear skirts in labor, they wore mainly trousers. Their clothes were characterized by bright red and green, just like the saying "people dressed in red until their forties, and in green when they are old".

In the early days after the founding of PRC, blue or gray cadres' suit (men and women with the same style) became very popular, and even the elderly men and women felt very proud of wearing cadres' suit. Since the reform and opening up, with various dress styles, the young men and women became more and more

新县彭氏宗祠（信阳学院冯葆炜摄影）
Ancestral Hall of the Peng Family in Xinxian County
(Photography by Feng Baowei, Xinyang University)

过去信阳的住房多为砖木结构和土木结构，一般坐北朝南。在山区和河边的，则依山势和水势而建。现在农村建房一般是砖混结构的二层小楼。集镇盖楼房主要以做生意为主，居住为次，一般上、下二层，一层做生意，二层居住。城镇社区住宅特点是靠公路沿线盖门面房，既住人又经商。

fashionable, wearing clothes in different colors and styles, in keeping with Chinese and global fashion trends. The dress style in Xinyang is the representation of the fashion trend.

(2) Housing

Xinyang people have their own customs in their housing. House building is a big event for one family, and relatives, friends and neighbors always come to help. When the house is set up, they will send some gifts and congratulations.

Due to the different customs in the counties, the buildings in southern Henan were summarized as "armed ridge and six beasts". The ridge of the house was decorated with some animal carvings, such as tiger, lion, dragon, deer, sheep, etc., made by clay, known as "armed ridge". The ridge of the front door was also carved with some wild beasts as tiger or lion, like military officers protecting the house. The ridges of the living rooms on both sides of the front door were carved with fish, pigeon or crane, symbolizing peace, auspice, luck and longevity respectively. But, the family with low standard of living used "civil ridge", also called "loach ridge", the ridge without any decorations or animal carvings.

In the past, the houses in Xinyang were mostly made by wood or bricks,

信阳浉河区楼畈村（信阳学院冯春晓摄影）
Loufan Village in Shihe District, Xinyang(Photography by Feng Chunxiao, Xinyang University)

信阳睡仙桥村：沿街而建的商住混合建筑（信阳师范学院辛文迪摄影）
Residential and Commercial Buildings in Shuixianqiao Village, Xinyang
(Photography by Xin Wendi, Xinyang Normal University)

（3）行

"行"的民俗主要体现在出行方式和出行禁忌方面。

新中国成立前，信阳地区人们的出行习惯主要是步行和乘船，近途的步行，远途的乘船。淮河上游支流众多，淮河和多数支流都是通航的，一般都是私人航运，设有码头，便于人们出行。官宦和乡绅出行一般是乘坐轿子，像北方那样骑马、骑驴的比较少。

在过去，人们出远门旅行前是要"看日子"的，选一个所谓的"黄道吉日"方可出行，尤以商贾最为讲究。经商人一般选择双日出门，双日又以四、六、八日为佳；单日中逢三、九为凶日。故此，俗有"初三、十三、二十三，姥姥给马不去牵"之说。一般人也有"七不出门，八不回家"之说。

新中国成立后，除淮滨、固始等地之外，淮河上游的多数支流不再通航，取而代之的是20世纪70—90年代的骑自行车、摩托车，开拖拉机，乘长途汽车等。现在，信阳的高铁十分方便，尽管有四通八达的高速公路，还有明港机场，但人们还是更习惯乘坐火车（高铁）远行，而由于私家车的普及，自驾出行已成了新俗。

generally with the door facing the south. Those in the mountains and by the rivers were built according to the mountains' positions and the water flow. Now the rural house building is generally a two-storied building made of brick and concrete. The two-storied house buildings in the countryside have dual purposes: business on the first floor and living on the second floor. The house building in towns is always located on the side of the highway for both living and business.

(3) Transportation

The customs on transportation mainly lie in the way of getting around and its taboos.

Before the founding of PRC, Xinyang people got around mainly on foot for a short trip and by boat for a long one. There were many tributaries in the upper reaches of the Huaihe River. The Huaihe River and most of its tributaries were navigable for private shipping, with docks to travel. Officials and squires usually traveled in sedan chairs. Few people rode horses or donkeys like those in the north.

In the past, people, especially the businessmen, had to "pick up the date", choosing a so-called "auspicious day" before going on a long trip. The businessmen generally chose the dates with even numbers to go out, among which the dates with the number four, six and eight in every month were preferred; while the dates with the number three and nine were considered unlucky. Therefore, a saying went that "on the third, thirteenth and twenty-third of the month, one wouldn't go outside even the grandma asked to do", and there was also a taboo "neither going outside on the seventh nor returning home on the eighth" prevalent among the common people.

After the founding of PRC, except Huaibin and Gushi counties, most of the tributaries of the upper reaches of the Huaihe River were no longer navigable. Then, it was popular to get around by bicycle, motorcycle, tractor and long-distance bus etc. between the 1970s and the 1990s. Nowadays, since it is very convenient for Xinyang people to travel by high-speed train, people prefer to use it for long distances, although there are expressways in all directions as well as the Minggang airport. With the popularization of private cars, self-driving is also an option.

二、社会生活民俗

社会生活民俗主要指社会组织的民俗、岁时节日的民俗和人生各个阶段的礼俗。在豫南，岁时节日民俗和人生礼俗最具特色，与河南其他区域很不相同。

1. 岁时节日民俗

中国人向来重视节日，非常尊重节日民俗，特别是一些老年人更是"不敢越雷池半步"，淮河上游地区的豫南也是这样。但由于这里是"歌舞之乡"，在岁时节日民俗中，歌和舞的成分比别的地方更重一些。

（1）除夕和春节

除夕和春节是一年中相毗连的两个大节。除夕阖家团圆的日子，不管有多远，不管做什么差事，这一天一定要赶回家。年三十下午就要准备晚饭菜肴，包饺子。晚上全家欢聚一起，举行丰盛的家宴，祭奠列祖列宗，入夜后在祖宗牌位前点烛、焚香直至天明。在没有电视没有手机的年代，全家老少围坐火塘说笑、唱歌，俗称"守岁"，戏之为"守棉袄"。五更时分，家长沐浴更换新衣、新帽、新鞋袜，都想抢先放鞭炮，然后礼拜祖宗、天地，迎接财神、喜神、灶神，称之为"接年"。小孩们新衣新鞋新帽，给大人们拜年，接压岁钱。

守岁年俗（信阳师范学院辛文迪摄影）
Folk Custom of *Shou Sui* (Photography by Xin Wendi, Xinyang Normal University)

II. Folk Customs on Social Life

The customs on social life mainly refer to those of social organizations, of the festivals during the year, and the customs during various stages of one's life. In southern Henan Province, the latter two customs are the most distinctive, and are quite different from those in other areas of Henan Province.

1. Festivals During the Year

Chinese people, especially the old, always take lunar festivals and traditional customs seriously. They never violate the routine of traditional customs. The same is true in southern Henan Province, the upper reaches of the Huaihe River. As "the hometown of singing and dancing", Xinyang pays more attention to singing and dancing on festivals during the year than other places.

(1) Chinese Lunar New Year's Eve and the Spring Festival

Chinese Lunar New Year's Eve and the Spring Festival are two major festivals linking the passing year and the following new year. Lunar New Year's Eve is the day for family reunion. No matter how far from home and how busy one is, he/she must get home on that day. In the afternoon of the Lunar New Year's Eve, each family is busy preparing dinner and making *jiaozi*. In the evening, the whole family get together, hold a memorial ceremony for ancestor worship, and feast on dinner. At night, candles and incense are lit until dawn in front of the ancestral memorial tablets. In the days when there was no TV or mobile phone, the whole family sat around the fire and stayed up late or whole night, talking, laughing and singing, commonly known as *Shou Sui*, or jokingly called "awaiting *mian'ao*". After a bath at about the fifth watch (3-5 a.m.), parents would wear new clothes, new hats, new shoes and socks. They all strove to be the first to set off firecrackers. And then, they worshiped their ancestors, the Heaven and the Earth. They greeted the God of Wealth, the God of Joy and the God of Fire warmly, which was known as "Welcoming the New Year". Children all wore new clothes, new shoes and new hats and sent New Year's greetings to adults, for receiving New Year's lucky money.

The first day of the first lunar month is the Spring Festival. In the morning, when the *jiaozi* is ready, the family enjoy it after worshiping ancestors and gods.

正月初一是春节，是新年，早晨下好饺子，先敬祖先神明，然后一家人才能吃饺子。早饭后，人们开始敲锣打鼓往湾邻拜年，每到一家都要唱锣鼓唱（即以锣鼓伴奏唱民歌）。初二以后，要带点心、酒、腊肉、粉条等礼品，在主要亲朋之间相互走动拜年，见面要相互问好，唱吉祥的民歌，一般到正月十三为止。

（2）正月十五

农家历来重视元宵节，素有"正月十五大似年"之说。节日这天，各家举行早餐宴，早餐抢早，象征早种早收，晚饭吃水饺。黄昏，家家户户去坟山给祖先送灯以示纪念，"圆亮"（灯火全部都点着）之后，山坡上灯光成排成行，横竖交错，十分好看壮观。入夜，各村、各湾组织民间艺人举行玩狮子、划旱船、跑竹马、踩高跷、下地灯、舞彩龙等文艺活动，家家户户彩灯高挂，室内灯火通明，通宵达旦，民间称之为"观灯"。

（3）端阳节

端阳节早餐吃粽子，并以数个抛撒河、塘、湖、库之中，表示对楚国大诗人屈原的祭奠和怀念。门窗上两角各插艾蒿一根，象征去风避邪。

民间脸谱灯笼（信阳学院冯春晓摄影）
Folk Mask Lantern (Photography by Feng Chunxiao, Xinyang University)

And then, people greet the village neighbors for the Spring Festival by beating gongs and drums. They sing folk songs at every house they visit. On the second day, they bring snacks, wine, preserved meat, starch noodles and other gifts to visit close relatives and friends, greeting each other and singing auspicious folk songs for each other. Generally, this lasts until the 13th day of the first lunar month.

(2) The 15th Day of the First Lunar Month

Farmers have always attached importance to the Lantern Festival, which has long been regarded as important as the day of the lunar New Year's Eve. On this day, each family holds their breakfast banquet as early as possible, symbolizing early planting and early harvesting, and eats *jiaozi* for dinner. At dusk, each family visits ancestral graves and sends lights in memory of them. When the lights are all lit, it is spectacular to see the rows of lights on the hillside. At night, each village will enjoy some cultural activities by local artisans, such as lion dancing, rowing land boats, running bamboo horses, walking on stilts, ground lanterns and dragon dancing. Colored lanterns are hung from house to house and lit all night, which is known as "watching lanterns".

(3) Dragon Boat Festival

People usually have *zongzi* (glutinous rice wrapped in bamboo leaves) for breakfast on the Dragon Boat Festival, and throw some into the river, pond or lake to honour Qu Yuan, the great poet of the Chu State. A bunch of felon herb on both sides of the door and the window keeps people away from sickness and evilness. During the festival, people entertain each other. Newlyweds are invited by the bride's parents to celebrate the festival, which is called the "New Dragon Boat Festival". Meanwhile, married girls of all generations are also invited to reunite with their parents.

(4) Mid-Autumn Festival

On Mid-Autumn Festival, all families grind fresh glutinous rice into flour and make *tangyuan* (glutinous rice balls) or steamed buns as the main food. *Tangyuan*, commonly known as "soup cake", is often stewed with pork, chicken, duck and goose meat. Sesame and beans are commonly used as the stuffing of steamed buns. After the founding of PRC, most families also buy some mooncakes, pastries, sweets and so on to celebrate the festival. At night, families sit outside together to admire the full moon, and enjoy delicious food such as

端阳节也是人们相互交往宴请之节,新婚夫妇都要被女方娘家请去过节,称之为"新端阳",出嫁的各辈姑娘,也被娘家请去团聚。

(4)中秋节

中秋节各家各户用新鲜糯米磨成粉,做成汤圆或糍馍馍作为节日主食。汤圆俗称"羹粑",多伴猪、鸡、鸭、鹅肉炖食;糍馍馍多用芝麻、豆类作馅。新中国成立后,多数人家也购些月饼、糕点、糖果之类过节。入夜,阖家团聚,赏月,吃板栗、花生、瓜子、糕点等,共庆丰收。

2. 人生礼俗

人生礼俗主要指人的诞生、生日、婚姻、丧葬等人生历程方面的习俗。

(1)诞生、洗三习俗

农耕社会,人就是生产力,故而特别重视生育,因为多生多育被视为人丁兴旺的盛事,尤其喜欢生男孩,故有"五子登科""七子团圆""十子全福"等"多子多福"的美好愿望。

旧时在豫南,凡生第一胎婴儿,须立即向岳丈家报喜,岳父母将早已准备好的小孩衣物、母鸡等交报喜人带回,在婴儿出生后的七至十天内将"月礼"送到男方家里。婴儿"三朝"这天,要给婴儿起乳名,洗澡穿衣,因此三朝又叫"洗三",有复杂的程序。婴儿满月,产妇抱着婴儿走娘家,名曰"吃满月盐"。

(2)周岁习俗

当小孩儿长到一周岁,不论家庭是穷是富,都要为小孩儿过周岁生日,名曰"抓周"。这一天,亲朋好友聚在一起,在桌子上摆各种日常用品、文房四宝和一些象征性的物品,让小孩子任意抓取,抓到某种东西,就象征着这个孩子长大要干某一行事业。这当然只是一种习俗,抓周是图个吉利。亲友们即兴编词,唱吉祥祝福的民歌。

chestnuts, peanuts, melon seeds, cakes and pastries to celebrate the harvest.

2. Rituals and Customs on Life

Life rituals and customs mainly refer to those about people's birth, birthday, marriage, funeral, etc. in our life.

(1) Customs on Celebrating Birth and the Third Day of the Birth

In an agricultural society, since people are the labor forces, they take child birth seriously. More child birth, especially baby boy, is regarded as the great event of prosperity. Therefore, such expressions as "five sons passing the imperial examinations", "seven sons reuniting with their parents", "ten sons bringing all happiness" etc. are deeply rooted in people's minds which imply people's good wishes of "more sons, more happiness".

In the old days, when the first baby was born in southern Henan, the good news must immediately be reported to the wife's parents, and the parents would ask the person who brought the news to take those gifts, including the baby's clothes and hens back. In seven to ten days after the birth, the "month gifts" would be sent to the man's home. On the third day of the birth, there was a seemingly complex procedure: the baby would be given a pet name, take a bath and be dressed, which was also called "the third-day bath after birth". When the baby was a full month old, the mother would take the baby to her parents' home, which was called "savoring the full-month salt".

(2) One-year-old Customs

When a baby is one year old, no matter whether the family is rich or poor, the first birthday ceremony must be held, which is called *Zhuazhou* (baby's random choice of different presents with symbolic significance). On this day, friends and relatives get together, put a variety of daily necessities, the four treasures of study (writing brush, ink stick, ink slab and paper in the study of a scholar) and some symbolic items on the table, and let the baby grab them at will. When the baby catches any item, it symbolizes that the baby will do a certain business after growing up. This is of course just a custom, wishing for good luck. Meanwhile, friends and relatives improvise lyrics and sing auspicious and blessing folk songs.

(3) Marriage Customs

The wedding etiquette in southern Henan is complicated, including

洗三（信阳师范学院辛文迪绘画）
The Third-day Bath after Birth (Drawn by Xin Wendi, Xinyang Normal University)

（3）婚嫁习俗

豫南的婚嫁礼仪繁杂，主要有定亲、择吉、备婚、过礼和嫁娶等程序。男女双方了解对方情况后都满意，可以定亲，之后择吉日，接着准备结婚用品，婚礼前几天，男方要备重礼送至女方家中，随后就是迎娶环节。迎娶分为迎亲和送亲两种形式。

期间每一个环节都要唱歌，其中入洞房时的"撒帐歌"最有特点，闹洞房时"锣鼓唱"最为热闹。

（4）丧葬习俗

丧葬习俗是一个地区自然、经济、文化的某种反映，豫南淮河上游各地的丧葬礼俗有一定的差别，其中，以光州的丧葬礼俗最为完整，较能反映本区域民众的信仰、禁忌等精神世界概貌。主要习俗有发讣告（或报丧）和报庙，招煞和十念，祭亡堂，谢孝等。

engagement, picking the auspicious day, marriage preparation, presenting betrothal gifts and marriage. After a full understanding and falling in love with each other, the boy and the girl could get engaged, choose an auspicious day, and then prepare for the wedding. A few days before the wedding, the boy should present lavish gifts to the girl's home. The wedding procedure includes two parts: the groom's procession of receiving the bride and the bridal procession of seeing the bride off.

During each part people will sing songs, among which "Sazhang songs" (a wedding custom to sing songs when throwing different items with symbolic significance into the bed net on the bed) is the most important when entering the bridal chamber, while singing to the gongs and drums is the liveliest when celebrating wedding in the bridal chamber.

(4) Funeral Rituals and Customs

Funeral customs are a reflection of regional nature, economy and culture. There are certain differences in funeral customs in the upper reaches of the Huaihe River in southern Henan. Among them, the funeral customs in Guangzhou (present Huangchuan County, Henan Province) are the most complete and can better reflect the spiritual life of local people. The rituals and customs mainly include: giving obituaries (or announcing the death) and reporting the death to the earth temple, *Qiasha* (a *Feng Shui* master or geomancer to see the cemetery and set the date of the funeral) and *Shinian* (generally four Taoists to sing along with musical instruments to open the way for the dead), sacrificing the dead, and *Xiexiao* (the filial offspring to pay tribute to the mourners).

三、精神生活民俗

精神生活民俗主要指游艺民俗和民俗观念。游艺民俗包含民间游戏、竞技、社火等娱乐活动；民俗观念则反映在一个地域的民间信仰、民间传说、民间故事、谚语里。

信阳地区，淮河穿境而过，中原文化与吴楚文化在这里交汇融合，成就了她文风昌盛、艺术繁茂、民风淳朴的区域文化特征。"歌舞之乡"歌舞之多样、道具之精细、表演之丰富，在淮河流域独树一帜，尤其是以歌舞为载体的游艺民俗——正月十五"花会""灯会"最具特色。

农历正月十五官称元宵节，是春节的节日气氛的最高点。为迎接元宵节，一般在春节前一个月就开始做准备，一些社会组织或商贾请来工匠师，扎花灯，做爆竹，制造烟火。农村一般以村落或家族为单位，制作龙灯、旱船、跑驴等灯节所用道具。从正月十四日晚上开始，一直到正月十七，到达灯会的高潮。期间，耍龙灯，舞狮子，跑旱船，挂花灯，燃鞭炮，放焰火，城乡一片灯的海洋、欢乐的海洋。

元宵节玩灯叫"出灯会"，分为"花会""正会"和"出全会"。

1. 花会

所谓花会，是指群众自发组织、自由表演、自娱娱人的歌舞、社火表演活动。花会的表演形式十分多样，主要有耍龙灯、舞狮子、扭角、台阁、跑旱船、打花滚、高跷、老背少、花车子、花挑、蚌壳舞、竹马灯、跑驴、花鼓灯、地灯戏、小放牛、地秧歌儿等等，一般都有歌唱，即兴喊唱出符合当时情景的唱词。

III. Folk Customs on Spiritual Life

Folk customs on spiritual life mainly refer to those concerning recreational arts and folk concepts. Folk arts include folk games, competitions, *Shehuo* (a general name for such celebration activities by the folk artisans as described above, such as lion dance and dragon dance, rowing land boats, running bamboo horses, walking on stilts, etc.) and other recreational activities. The concept of folk customs is reflected in the regional folk beliefs, legends, stories and proverbs.

The Huaihe River runs through Xinyang area, and the cultures of the Central Plains and that of Wu & Chu states coalesce here, which contributes to her simple regional cultural characteristics: extravagant writing, lush art, and rustic folkway. Xinyang, known as "the land of songs and dances", is unique in the Huaihe River Basin for its variety of songs and dances, elaborate props and rich performances. In particular, the "Lantern Parade" on the 15th day of the first lunar month is the most distinctive folk custom.

丰富多彩的信阳民俗文化表演
Colorful Folk Culture Performances in Xinyang

The 15th day of the first lunar month, known as the Lantern Festival, is the culmination of the festive atmosphere of the Spring Festival. To celebrate the Lantern Festival, people usually start to make preparations one month before the Spring Festival. Some social organizations or merchants invite artisans to make lanterns and fireworks. In rural areas, families or villages make props for

丁李湾地灯戏表演（蒋仑摄影）

Ground Lanterns Performance in Dingliwan Village（Photography by Jiang Lun）

2. 正会

正会又叫"胜会"，含有争胜、比赛之意。正会是有组织的花会形式，以街道或村庄为单位，组成花会队伍。如光州城关原来就有北城大街的"如意会"、南城东关的"永安会"、北城小东关的"长生会"，南城大巷街、曾家巷都有正会。每个正会都由头面人物出任"会首"，负责正会的各项工作，比如研究决定出什么样的花会项目，筹集资金购置、添加服装道具，组织人员排练演习，设计和制作"台阁"，等等。每一个正会都必须有一个玩花会的行家里手作为会首，才能把正会办好。

the Lantern Festival, such as dragon lanterns, land boats and running donkeys. From the 14th night of the first lunar month, until the 17th, the Lantern Festival will gradually reach the climax. During this period, lighting dragon lanterns, performing lion dance, running land boats, hanging lanterns, burning firecrackers and fireworks, people in urban and rural areas can enjoy the festival to the fullest, watching colorful lanterns, singing and laughing.

Lantern Festival celebration, also called Lantern Parade, is divided into Huahui, Zhenghui and Quanhui Play.

1. Huahui

Huahui refers to the singing and dancing, and Shehuo performances organized by the masses spontaneously and performed freely just for entertainment. There are diversified performances. Besides those forms described above, people can also enjoy watching horn-twist, Taige (kids playing on the stage with cleverly designed modeling and breathtaking effects), diversified rolling, the old carrying the young, Huatiao (flower-shouldering), mussel shell dance, hobbyhorse lanterns, racedonkey dance, Huagu (flower-drum), ground lanterns (no stage) performance, little cowboy dance, and yangko performance. The performers usually improvise to sing the lyrics in accordance with the situation at that time.

2. Zhenghui

Zhenghui, also called Formal Lantern Parade or Shenghui, means to win or compete in the performance. It is an organized parade form, with performing teams from different streets or villages, for example, "Ruyi Parade" "Yong'an Parade" and "Changsheng Parade", etc. holding respectively in north main street, and Daxiang street and Zengjia alley of south city in Guangzhou County. Each parade is headed by a prominent local, who is responsible for various work, such as deciding the kinds of performances, raising funds to purchase costumes and props, organizing rehearsals, designing and making Taige, and so on. In order to run the performance well, there must be an expert as its head in every parade.

3. 出全会

出全会就是所有的花会和正会，在农历正月十七这一天全部要上街表演，因为在信阳的民间传说中，农历正月十七是火神爷的寿诞之日。这一天，连同城隍爷、土地爷也一并祭拜，因此有的正会抬火神爷神像，有的抬城隍爷神像或土地爷神像。

这天上午，众人等将庙里的木质火神雕像抬出，前呼后拥将火神雕像抬到城南门外地藏庵行宫暂时安放，上供、朝拜、祈祷；午时一过，人们便抬着火神雕像，从地藏庵出来，一路浩浩荡荡进城。队伍的构成及顺序：开路先锋—牌灯—唢呐乐队—彩旗—宫灯—彩伞—捧灯—提灯—各种执事及各种花灯—台阁—乐队—龙棚、香炉—大轿、火神雕像—各种执事及花灯。当雕像经过时，人们纷纷磕头，祈求火神保佑新的一年风调雨顺、五谷丰登。队伍在县城里按一定的路线走走停停，接受人们的欢呼膜拜，直至火神庙或城隍庙或土地庙，将诸神送回，此时已是午夜时分。

3. Quanhui Play

Quanhui Play, or Whole Lantern Parade, means that all Huahui and Zhenghui have street performances on the 17th day of the first lunar month, because in Xinyang folklore, it is the birthday of the Fire God. On that day, the City God and the Earth God are also worshiped, so different teams will carry a different God in the parade.

In the morning, the crowd will carry the wooden statue of the Fire God to the Dizang Temple outside of the south city gate temporarily, offering, worshiping and praying; immediately after 12 o'clock, the crowd will carry the statue back into the city. The team is composed of trailbreaker, Suona band, colorful flags and umbrellas, Taige and different lanterns. These items are arranged in a strict order. As the statue of the God passes by, the crowd will kowtow and pray to the Fire God for good weather and a good harvest in the coming year. The procession takes a certain route through the county, accepting cheers and worship. It is not until midnight that the crowd sends each God back to the temple.

四、新民俗

如果说以上都是传统民俗的话,那么,新时期以来,豫南淮河流域又增添了一些新的民俗,其中影响最大的当属"茶叶节"民俗和"丰收节"民俗了。

1. "茶叶节"民俗

"茶叶节"全称"中国信阳茶叶节",创办于1992年,2010年更名为"中国茶都·信阳国际茶文化节"。迄今已连续举办29届的"茶叶节",已然成为当地的民俗。

"茶叶节"举办之时,当地政府投入大量资金完善硬件设施,优化营商环境;大大小小的酒店做好充分准备,迎接国内外茶商、游客、媒体的莅临;所有的饭馆、茶楼明窗净几,准备好充足的美食和上好的茶叶,等待着四面八方客人的到来;大街小巷彩旗招展,打扫得干净整洁。最繁忙、最热闹的地方当属一座座茶山,人们争分夺秒、昼夜不停地采茶、炒茶,一篓篓刚采下来的新鲜芽头,一夜之间就变成了香气四溢的信阳毛尖茶叶,源源不断地送到"茶叶节"的交易市场之中。

除了经贸活动,"茶叶节"期间,大型的开幕式、闭幕式文艺表演最令信阳人瞩目;丰富多彩的踩街活动,将传统民俗表演展现得淋漓尽致;民歌大赛、皮影戏演出、花鼓戏表演、焰火晚会等等,将豫南信阳装扮成了"人间最美四月天"。

2. "丰收节"民俗

淮河流域民众所说的"丰收节",即"中国农民丰收节",是第一个在国家层面专门为农民设立的节日。该节日设立自2018年,每年的农历秋分日即为"丰收节"。

IV. New Folk Customs

Nowadays, there are some new folk customs in the Huaihe River Basin in southern Henan, among which the most influential ones are "tea festival" and "harvest festival".

1. Tea Festival

"China Xinyang Tea Festival" as its full name, began in 1992. In 2010, it was renamed as "China Tea Capital·Xinyang International Tea Culture Festival". "Tea Festival", which has been held for 29 consecutive years, has already become a local folk custom.

When the "Tea Festival" is held, the local government will invest a lot of money to improve the hardware facilities and optimize the business environment. All the hotels make full preparations to welcome the tea merchants, tourists and media from China and abroad; all the bright and clean restaurants and teahouses have prepared ample food and good tea for the guests. The streets and alleys are lined with colorful flags. Each tea mountain is the busiest and most lively place. People race against time to pick and fry tea day and night. The fresh teabuds that have just been picked will become fragrant Xinyang Maojian tea overnight, which is continuously carried to the trading market of the "Tea Festival".

In addition to economic and trade activities, during the "Tea Festival", the large scale opening ceremony and closing ceremony are the most eye-catching performances to Xinyang people; colorful street activities including lion dance, land boats and yangko performances will show the traditional folk performances incisively and vividly; and those activities, like folk song contest, shadow play performance, Huagu (Flower-drum) opera and fireworks and so on, make Xinyang "the most beautiful place in April".

2. Harvest Festival

The "Harvest Festival" in the Huaihe River Basin is the first national festival dedicated to farmers. Established in 2018, the festival falls on the Autumn Equinox every year.

As one of the earliest rice-growing areas in China, the Huaihe River Basin

淮河流域作为中国最早的稻作区之一，自古以来就是以农为本的经济结构，进入新世纪以后，特别是党的十八大以来，淮河流域连年丰收，农民收入持续增加，各地经常举办庆祝丰收的活动。"中国农民丰收节"设立以来，更是极大地调动了农民的积极性、主动性和创造性。

中国信阳·大别山农民丰收节（潢川摄协肖乃宝摄影）
Dabie Mountain Farmer Harvest Festival, Xinyang, China (Photography by Xiao Naibao, Huangchuan Photographers Association)

每年的"丰收节"，各地都要举行丰富多彩的庆祝活动，农民们将丰收的粮食、瓜果、蔬菜等展示在活动当中，载歌载舞庆祝丰收；农业嘉年华、大众化的休闲观光成为节日亮点；广大市民在节日期间纷纷回归乡村，参与农事体验，品味农村情调和田园风光。

"丰收节"已成为新的民俗，它极大地提升了农民的荣誉感、幸福感和获得感，并不断推进着农业现代化进程。农业的绿色发展，农村改革、结构调整，脱贫攻坚成果，都在这新的民俗中得以展现并与之形成良性互动，展示着中国农村改革发展的巨大成就。

has had an agriculture-oriented economic structure since ancient times. Since the beginning of the 21st century, especially since the 18th National Congress of the Communist Party of China, the Huaihe River Basin has enjoyed bumper harvests in successive years and the farmers' incomes have continued to increase, hence harvest celebrations are common. The establishment of "Chinese Farmers Harvest Festival" has greatly aroused the enthusiasm, initiative and creativity of farmers.

During the annual "Harvest Festival", rich and colorful celebration activities are held everywhere. Farmers will display their grain, fruits, and vegetables, etc., singing and dancing to celebrate the harvest; agricultural carnival and mass sightseeing are the highlights of the festival. The majority of citizens have returned to the countryside during the festival to participate in farming, experience the rural sentiment, and enjoy the pastoral scenery.

丰收节上赛挑谷（信阳摄协蔺仲武摄影）
Rice Fetching Race in the Harvest Festival (Photography by Lin Zhongwu, Xinyang Photographers Association)

The "Harvest Festival" has become a new folk custom, which greatly improves farmers' sense of honor, happiness and sense of gain, while constantly promoting the agricultural modernization. The green development of agriculture, rural reform and structural adjustment, and the achievements of poverty alleviation are all displayed in this new folk custom and form a positive interaction, demonstrating the great achievements of China's rural reform and development.

第六章

音乐篇：淮河民间音乐文化

Chapter 6

Music: Folk Music Culture Along the Huaihe River

民间音乐是老百姓直接创造和使用的一种音乐艺术形式。它源于人民生活，又对人民生活起着广泛而深入的作用。淮河民间音乐的历史悠久，内容丰富，形式多样，其中最富有地域特色的是这里的民歌、民间舞蹈和仪式戏剧。2006 年，固始花挑入选河南省首批非物质文化遗产名录；2008 年，信阳民歌被列入第二批国家级非物质文化遗产名录；2019 年，罗山县文化馆因"罗山皮影"被列为国家级非物质文化遗产代表性项目保护单位。

一、唱着过的岁月：民间歌曲

民间歌曲是劳动者的歌，是人们世世代代一脉相承、传唱不息的生活之歌。它们充分展示了先民们的创造智慧和艺术才华，生动体现了先民们美好而丰富的精神世界，概括反映出了先民们在不同历史时期生息劳作的生活场景，真实地表达了先民们喜怒哀乐的情感世界和鲜明的审美取向。

1. 自然的歌：山歌

"山歌"是人们对那些曲调高亢嘹亮，节奏自由自在，歌词多是即兴创作，情感表达朴实、直接的歌曲的统称，中国各地的山歌都有自己的名字，是当地老百姓对它们的"爱称"。

淮河流域山歌主要集中在淮河上游，名称也非常有趣，被称为"五句子""慢赶牛""隔山应"，其中"五句子"最有特色，它的歌词既不是中国北方民歌的"上下句"两句体，也不是江南民歌的"起承转合"四句体，而是一种五句体结构，前四句用比兴手法，有起承转合的韵味，最后一句起到画龙点睛的作用。

Folk music is an art form created and used directly by the common people. It originates from people's life, and plays an extensive and profound role in popular culture. Folk music along the Huaihe River has a long history, rich content, and diverse forms, among which folk songs, folk dances and ritual dramas are the most distinctive in this region. In 2006, Gushi Flower-shouldering ("Huatiao" in Chinese) dance was selected into the first batch of Intangible Cultural Heritage List in Henan Province. In 2008, folk songs of Xinyang were included in the second batch of National Intangible Cultural Heritage List; in 2019, Luoshan County Cultural Center was enlisted as the representative project protection unit of National Intangible Cultural Heritage because of "Luoshan shadow play".

I. Years Full of Songs: Folk Songs

Folk songs are the songs of laborers and the songs about people's life that have been handed down from generation to generation. They fully demonstrate the creative wisdom and artistic talent of the predecessors, vividly reflect the beautiful and rich spiritual world of our predecessors, generally reflect the life scenes of the predecessors in different historical periods, and truly express their emotional world and distinct aesthetics orientation.

1. Songs of Nature: Mountain Songs

The term "mountain songs" does not literally refer to the songs only sung in the mountains, but a kind of folk song usually sung in the fields during or after work by the laborers. It is a general term for the songs with loud and clear tunes, free rhythms, improvising lyrics, and simple and direct emotional expressions. Mountain songs in different parts of China have their own "pet names" by the local people.

The mountain songs in the Huaihe River Basin are mainly popular in the upper reaches, which have very interesting names such as "five sentences", "slow cattle herding", and "a response over a mountain". The structure of "five sentences" is the most distinctive: its lyrics are neither the two-sentence structure of the folk songs in Northern China as "the above and the next lines", nor the four-sentence structure of Jiangnan folk songs as "Qi-Cheng-Zhuan-He", but a five-sentence

民歌对唱（信阳学院冯春晓摄影）
Folk Song Performance（Antiphonal Singing）(Photography by Feng Chunxiao, Xinyang University)

2. 劳动的歌：号子、田歌

号子即劳动号子，是人们在劳动时根据劳动用力的节律，自然发出的吆喝声。

淮河上的劳动号子都与河流相关，有加固河堤的打夯号子、石硪号子，有船运的摇橹号子、撑篙号子、拉纤号子、架包号子、搬运号子，还有捕鱼的赶鱼号子等。淮河上的号子旋律性较强，音乐结构比较简单，节奏多与劳动节奏相呼应，歌词具有较强即兴性，多用衬词哟、嗬、哎、嗨等，具有一唱众和的特点。

田歌是淮河两岸农人从事田间劳动时集体演唱的民歌。田歌曲调优美流畅，节奏较为舒缓，歌词多半具有即兴性，少量歌词有叙事性。每年插秧季节，淮河边上就成了歌的海洋，歌声此起彼伏，汇成一首壮美的田园大合唱，真是美不胜收。

随着生产、生活方式的改变，淮河上的号子和田歌几成绝响。

structure, in which metaphor is applied in the first four sentences functioning similarly as "Qi-Cheng-Zhuan-He", and the last sentence makes the finishing touch.(Note: "Qi-Cheng-Zhuan-He" means the structural principle of ethnic music. "Qi" is the initial statement of the theme, "Cheng" consolidates the theme through repetition, "Zhuan" develops the theme, and "He" is to finish the music.)

2. Labor Songs: Chanties and Field Songs

Chanty is the natural shout people make according to the laboring rhythm.

Chanty on the Huaihe River is all related to the river, such as the tamping chanty for river bank reinforcement, chanty of yuloh, punting, and boat towing, handling chanty for shipping, and finally, fishing chanty. Usually, one person leads the chanty and the others sing along. The chanties have a relatively strong melody and a simple structure, with the rhythm echoing with the labor rhythm. The lyrics are mostly improvised, using the padding syllables such as yo, ho, ai, hi, etc.

Field songs are a kind of folk songs sung by the farmers on both sides of the Huaihe River when they are engaged in field work. The melody is beautiful and smooth, with a relatively slow rhythm. Most of the lyrics are improvised, with only some being narrative. Every year in the rice planting season, there would be a sea of songs along the banks of the Huaihe River, presenting in front of us a magnificent rural chorus.

信阳民歌国家级传承人胡大坤在田间唱情歌（信阳学院冯春晓摄影）
Field Song Performed by Hu Dakun (right), National Inheritor of Xinyang Folk Songs
((Photography by Feng Chunxiao, Xinyang University)

3. 生活的歌：小调、灯歌

如果说山歌是"山野之歌"，那么小调则是"里巷之曲"，它经过了整理加工，有了相对固定的唱词和曲调，还有的加入了伴奏，成为委婉动听、内容丰富、形式完整的民歌。淮河的小调数量很多，小调的内容以家长里短、诉苦、相思为主，还有一部分叙事性小调，讲述相对完整的小故事或民间传说。

灯歌是由田歌演变而来的颇具地域风格的民间艺术，多在元宵佳节时表演。四周花灯高照，中间画地为台，表演时一生一旦演唱，锣鼓击节，观众帮腔。灯歌节奏鲜明，旋律流畅，结构与田歌相近，属于双句式，一般都有完整的故事情节，表演性和观赏性强。

小调和灯歌的内容最丰富，包罗了淮河民众日常生活的诸方面。

潢川民间歌唱家在表演（信阳学院冯春晓摄影）
The Performance of Folk Singer from Huangchuan County
(Photography by Feng Chunxiao, Xinyang University)

4. 革命的歌：红色民歌

红色民歌在革命战争年代起到了宣传革命、组织群众、鼓舞斗志的作用。目前采集整理的红色民歌，主要是由当年亲历过革命战争的老红军和当地民众口头传唱而流传下来的。

With the change of work and life style, the chanties and field songs on the Huaihe River have become far less common.

3. Songs of Life: Popular Tunes and Lantern Songs

Popular tunes are a genre of Chinese folk songs. If mountain songs are the "songs in the mountains and fields", then popular tunes are the "songs in the streets and lanes". After continuous improvement and supplement, they have relatively fixed lyrics and tunes, some of which have added accompaniment, becoming beautiful and melodious folk songs with rich contents and complete forms. There are a large number of popular tunes on the Huaihe River mainly concerning household affairs, complaints and lovesickness, as well as some narrative tunes telling complete short stories or folklore.

The lantern song is a kind of folk art with a regional style evolved from the field song. It is often performed during the Lantern Festival without any stages. With lanterns hanging high, one male character and one female character are singing to the gongs and drums, with the audience singing along. The lantern song has a distinct rhythm and a smooth melody. Its structure is similar to that of the field song, namely, the two-sentence structure. It generally has a complete storyline, being highly performative and ornamental.

Popular tunes and lantern songs have the most abundant content, covering all aspects of people's daily life along the Huaihe River.

4. Songs of Revolution: Red Folk Songs

Red folk songs played the role of publicizing the revolution, organizing the masses and inspiring morale in the revolutionary years. At present, the red folk songs that have been collected and sorted mainly refer to those passed down orally by the old Red Army soldiers and local people who have ever been involved in the revolutionary war.

During the first and second domestic revolutionary wars (respectively 1924-1927 and 1927-1937), people in southern Henan took part in the revolutions, singing such songs as *Long-term Hired Hands* and *A Tune of the Poor*; with the continuous growth and development of the Hubei-Henan-Anhui Revolutionary Base and the Fourth Red Army, they created a large number of red folk songs

第一次、第二次国内革命战争时期,豫南人民唱着《长工歌》《穷人调》参加革命;随着鄂豫皖革命根据地和红四方面军的不断壮大,他们又唱出了《红旗插遍大别山》《送郎当红军》《红四军南下胜利歌》等一大批红色民歌,迎来全中国的解放。而淮河流域最著名的红色民歌当属那首红遍全国的《八月桂花遍地开》了!

　　淮河流域的民间歌曲歌唱自然,歌唱历史,歌唱社会,歌唱人生,唱出了一代代淮河儿女的心声。特别是信阳民歌,质朴优美、热情大方,许多知名歌唱家如吴雁泽、张也等,都曾演唱过信阳民歌或用信阳民歌曲调创作的新民歌。

such as *Red Flags Spreading Over the Dabie Mountains*, *Seeing My Husband Off to the Red Army*, *Victories by the Fourth Red Army Southward*, etc., ushering in the entire liberation of China, among which the most famous one in the Huaihe River Basin is *Osmanthus Flowers Blooming Everywhere in August*, a song popular all over China.

  The folk songs in the Huaihe River Basin are sung in praise of nature, history, society and life, expressing the aspirations of generations of the local people, especially those simple, beautiful, warm and generous Xinyang folk songs. Many famous singers, such as Wu Yanze and Zhang Ye, etc., have sung Xinyang folk songs or new folk songs created with Xinyang folk tunes.

二、淮水"三花":民间舞蹈

淮河流域民间舞蹈源远流长,从目前掌握的资料看,最早可追溯至西周以前的"巫舞"。历史学家吴晗在《我国古代舞蹈的发展情况》一文中说:"至今流行在淮河流域一带的花鼓灯舞,和流行在云南一带的花灯戏,舞人都是以手巾和扇子作为不可少的舞具,可能就是古代巾舞和鞞舞遗风的流传。"

淮河流域民间舞蹈形式多样,内容丰富,但最引人注目的大概要属花鼓灯、花挑舞和花伞舞了,合称淮水"三花"。

1. 淮河上的"东方芭蕾":花鼓灯

花鼓灯是淮河流域家喻户晓、老幼皆知的民间舞蹈艺术,是一种载歌载舞并与唱、帮、打三位一体相融合的民间舞蹈艺术。由于其表演难度大,又有"起蓬子"(女演员站在男演员肩膀上)表演,因此被誉为"东方芭蕾"。

花鼓灯有三种角色:一是老竿,或者叫竿头、伞头、伞把子;二是花鼓架子,或者叫挎、花鼓腿子;三是花鼓娘子,或者叫腊花、兰花、梳。表演时,四名(或八名)花鼓腿子击打花鼓或敲击鼓槌,四名(或八名)花鼓娘子手持折扇、手绢或击打小铜,在一名(或两名)高举"火伞"的老竿的带领下,变换各种队形进行表演。

老艺人们把花鼓灯的表演归纳为"傲头旦角,低头丑角",意思就是花鼓娘子的头要昂起来,动作奔放泼辣,性格热情大方;老竿与花鼓腿子则要低头哈腰、舞步轻快,小腿要有弹性,从而使上身和头部的动作保持微颤,以表现其人物的欢快、风趣和幽默的性格。老竿的站、立都是以猴子的动作形象为基本动态,十分机灵可爱。花鼓腿子的动作不但要表现其诙谐幽默的一面,同时还要表现其刚健挺拔的男子汉气概的

II. "Three Flowers" Along the Huaihe River: Folk Dances

The folk dances in the Huaihe River Basin boast of her long history, which can be traced back to the "sorcery dance" before the Western Zhou Dynasty. In his article *On the Development of Ancient Chinese Dance*, the Chinese historian Wu Han held that, "Both in the Huagu Dance popular so far in the Huaihe River Basin and the Lantern Opera popular in Yunnan Province, the dancers use towels and fans as indispensable dancing props, which is probably the inheritance of the ancient Towel Dance and Bing Dance (a kind of sorcery dance with sheepskin drum as the sole prop popular probably from the Han Dynasty)."

There are various forms and contents of folk dances in the Huaihe River Basin, but perhaps the most eye-catching ones are Huagu Dance, Huatiao Dance and Huasan Dance, collectively known as "Three Hua (Flowers)" on the Huaihe River.

1. "Oriental Ballet" on the Huaihe River: Huagu Dance

Huagu Dance is a well-known folk dance along the Huaihe River Basin, integrating singing, vocal accompaniment, and beating gongs and drums. Because of its difficult performance, for example, an actress performing on the shoulders of a male actor, it is also known as "oriental ballet".

There are three kinds of characters in Huagu Dance: Lao Gan (leading funny figure in the performance), Huagu Leg (funny figure in the performance) and Huagu Lady. During the performance, four (or eight) Huagu Legs hit drums or drumsticks, and four (or eight) Huagu Ladies, holding the folding fans and handkerchiefs, or hitting small gongs, change various formations under the guidance of one Lao Gan or two.

Elder artisans summed up the performance in Huagu Dance as "the female characters holding heads up, while the clowns lowering heads", which means that Huagu Ladies should hold their heads up, acting boldly and showing their generous characters; while Lao Gan and Huagu Legs bend their heads and dance enthusiastically, keeping the upper bodies and heads slightly quivering, so as to show their cheerful, funny and humorous character. The standing posture of the

一面，很多动作借鉴了武术的技巧，不仅丰富了舞蹈语汇，也大大增强了花鼓灯的观赏性。

潢川县民间艺人在表演花鼓灯（又称火淋子）（信阳学院冯葆伟摄影）
Huagu Opera Perfermance by Huangchuan Folk Artisans(Photography by Feng Baowei, Xinyang University)

"火伞"是花鼓灯最重要的道具，一般是用竹子和彩绸、彩纸扎成，一圈用红绸围住，四方各加一飘带，上方扎成莲花状，莲花中间有一灯心，老竿一手持"火伞"，一手拿破芭蕉扇。花鼓娘子一般左手拿花巾，右手持折扇；有的地方是拿着小铜锣进行舞蹈。花鼓腿子在早先都身挎花鼓，后因不便舞蹈，就弃鼓不挎，改为敲击鼓槌，只在固始县仍保留着身挎花鼓的传统和形式。

花鼓灯的音乐可分为三个部分。

一是打击乐部分，一般由花鼓、大锣、马锣和手锤组成，重要场合增加大锣、老钹和大堂鼓。常用打击乐曲牌有老三番、小五番、长流水、长锤、三锤、三番锣鼓、三清锣鼓、栀子花等。表演中，动作和锣鼓点相对固定。

二是灯歌部分，有花鼓灯调和歌舞音乐两种。花鼓灯调气氛热烈欢快，融唱、帮、打于一体，唱词有一定的即兴性；歌舞音乐又分民间小

Lao Gan imitates the movements and images of monkeys, clever and lovely. The movements of Huagu Legs are not only humorous, but also vigorous and manly. Many movements draw on the skills of martial arts, which not only enrich the vocabulary of dance, but also greatly enhance the appreciation of Huagu Dance.

The "fire umbrella" is the most important prop of Huagu Dance. It is usually made of bamboo, colored silk and paper, and is surrounded by red silk, with four ribbons on each side. It takes on the shape of a lotus flower at the top, with a lamp wick in the center. Lao Gan holds a "fire umbrella" and a broken palm-leaf fan, the Huagu Lady usually holds a towel in her left hand and a folding fan in her right. In some places, Huagu Ladies dance with small brass gongs, and Huagu Legs carry drums. Later on, they find it inconvenient to dance, so they abandon the Huagu drums and change to drumsticks. Only in Gushi County, the tradition and form of carrying drums is still retained.

The music for Huagu Dance can be divided into three sections.

Section 1. Percussion Music. Generally, it is composed of drums, gongs of various sizes and hand mallets. On some important occasions, there will be more big gongs, old cymbals and big tupans. There are many distinctive tune names for the percussion music. In the performance, the movements and the beating of gongs and drums are relatively fixed.

Section 2. Lantern Songs. Lantern songs can be classified into Huagu tunes and singing and dancing music. The former is warm and cheerful, with singing, vocal accompaniment and beating gongs and drums all in one, and the lyrics are improvised to a certain extent; and the latter is divided into folk ditties and drama music.

Section 3. Playlet Music. Playlet music mostly adopts the tunes and vocal music of the playlets with regional characteristics, such as *Kezi Opera* and *Huagu Lilac Opera*, and most of the music has been transformed to become an integral part of Huagu music.

Huagu Dance is characterized by its healthy and bright emotional colors, delicate in fierceness, charming in ruggedness, and tender in humor. It embodies the cultural characteristics along the Huaihe River Basin, as well as the character of people on both sides of the Huaihe River.

调和歌舞小戏音乐。

三是小戏音乐部分,多采用富有地域特色的地方小戏如咳子戏、花鼓丁香戏的音乐和唱腔,不过,大多已经花鼓灯化,成为花鼓灯音乐不可分割的组成部分。

花鼓灯健康明朗的感情色彩,泼辣中见细腻、粗犷中见妩媚、风趣中见柔情的风格,较集中地体现了淮河流域南北交融、刚柔相济的淮河文化特色和淮河两岸人民的性格特征。

2. 挑在肩上的信仰:花挑舞

花挑舞是淮河上游地区流行甚广的民间舞蹈,它的道具是一根细而软的竹制扁担,扁担上缠以彩纸,上用竹条扎制一弓形花蓬,扁担两端各悬挂一只扎满五颜六色纸花的竹篮,称作"花挑",表演时一女性担起"花挑"舞动,故名"花挑舞"或直接称"花挑"。

花挑舞是抒情三人舞,舞蹈动作有男女之间的挑逗、传情、爱慕等表现。演出形式有:节日里走街串巷;庭院表演;舞台表演——"踩场",即花挑姑娘一段彩扇独舞,然后引小丑和丫环出场。全花挑舞分三个段落。第一段是独舞(称"踩场"),包括"摆扇""端推扇""抱扇"等舞蹈动作;然后挑起花挑,双手聚拢花篮,以狮子滚绣球的动作连续翻身旋转,引小丑上场。舞蹈进入第二段,由小丑作"拧、腾、晃"的表演,和姑娘左右对转,双双用"扑蝶扇"引出丫环。第三段在别致的小锣声中,三人分前后左右跳"拜四门",尔后搭肩亮势唱小调;唱毕,三人嬉闹蹦耍,你追我赶,热闹非凡,结束舞蹈。

花挑舞的伴奏乐器均为打击乐,常用乐器有鼓、小镲、大镲、巴钩、马锣、大锣和小锣等;运用"闪板""闪鼓""闷锣""压鼓槌"的技巧变化,节奏跳跃、热烈、轻快。花挑舞所唱的小调为当地民歌,配合富有特色的舞蹈,显示出淮上人民的审美情趣。

信阳人表演的"火伞"舞（又称火淋子）（信阳学院冯春晓摄影）
Fire Umbrella Dance in Xinyang (Photography by Feng Chunxiao, Xinyang University)

2. Faith on the Shoulders: Huatiao Dance

Huatiao Dance is a popular folk dance in the upper reaches of the Huaihe River. The prop of this dance is a thin and soft bamboo shoulder pole, which is wrapped with colorful paper and tied with bamboo strips to make an arched canopy of flowers. Two bamboo baskets whose outer edge is covered with colorful paper flowers are hung at each end of the pole. This is the so-called "Huatiao". During the performance, a female dancer dances, shouldering the "Huatiao". Thus, it is called "Huatiao Dance", or simply "Huatiao", literally meaning "flower-shouldering dance".

Huatiao Dance is a lyrical pas de trois, unfolding such dance movements as teasing and conveying feelings of love between men and women. The dance can be performed on the streets during the festival, in the courtyard or on the stage. Huatiao Dance can be divided into three sections. In the first section, the Huatiao girl firstly performs a solo dance with a colorful fan on the stage (called Cai Chang), including the following movements: shaking the fan, pushing the fan, and holding the fan, etc. Then she shoulders the Huatiao and gathers the flower baskets with both hands, turning and spinning with the continuous lion

固始花挑舞（吴晓军摄影）
Huatiao Dance in Gushi County（Photography by Wu Xiaojun）

3. 花样装扮花样情结：花伞舞

淮上地区广泛流传的另一种民间歌舞就是花伞舞。早期的花伞舞是融合歌、舞、做于一体的地方小戏，叫作"刘二姐赶会"，又叫"一把伞"，由三人表演，一旦角持花伞，一个老头和一个老婆扮演父母随其左右，表演形式简单。新中国成立后，编创出"三把伞"，即老婆打一把伞居中，两位姑娘立其左右，各持一把伞平放两侧做车轮状，老头推车，另一姑娘拉车，推推拉拉、欢欢喜喜去赶会。

1958年时，人们又把"三把伞"改成了"六把伞"，参加信阳地区民间音乐舞蹈汇演，引起轰动，中央歌舞团、海政歌舞团、空政歌舞团等十几个文艺团体先后到信阳学习此节目。中央歌舞团于1959年参加维也纳世界青年联欢节演出荣获银质奖的《花伞舞》，就是由"六把伞"改编而成的。现在，花伞舞已演变为纯舞蹈，形式以少女群舞为主。

rolling hydrangea actions and ushering in the clown. In the second section, the clown, twisting his body, jumping and shaking on the stage, turns right and left together with the girl, both performing the fan movements of "flapping butterfly" to introduce the maid. In the third section, to the unique beat of a small gong, the three dance around to "worship four doors", and then sing ditty with hands on shoulders of each other. After that, they play happily and lovingly, dancing while chasing after one another. Finally, the dance comes to an end.

All the instruments for the dance are percussion instruments, and the commonly used ones are drum, small and big cymbals, gongs of various sizes, etc. Such techniques as "Shanban"(singing at intervals of the instrument beating), "Shangu" (singing at intervals of the drum beating), "Menluo" (quickly keeping the gong's surface steady with hand after beating) and "Yaguchui" (slower the beats of drumstick down) are used to make the jumping rhythm, lively and relaxed. The popular tunes of Huatiao Dance are the local folk songs, which are combined with the distinctive dance, showing the aesthetic taste of the people along the Huaihe River.

3. Ingenious Dress Up, Genuine Emotions: Flower Umbrella Dance

Flower Umbrella is pronounced "Huasan" in Chinese. It is another kind of folk dance widely spread in the upper reaches of the Huaihe River. In the early stages, it was a play that integrated song, dance and action, called "The 2nd Elder Sister Liu Attending the Temple Fair", or "An Umbrella". It was performed simply by three people: a girl and her "parents". The girl holds an umbrella, accompanied by an old man and an old lady acting as her parents. After the founding of PRC, the dance "Three Umbrellas" was created. In the performance, the old lady holds an umbrella in the center, and two girls stand on her both sides, each holding an umbrella to keep them even like the wheels, as if the old lady were sitting on the cart. The old man pushes the cart, and the other girl pulls it, going to the fair happily.

In 1958, the "Three Umbrellas" dance was adapted into "Six Umbrellas" and was performed in the Xinyang folk music and dance joint performance, creating quite a stir among the audiences. More than a dozen artistic groups, including the Central Song and Dance Troupe, the Song and Dance Troupe of the PLA

花伞舞（三把伞）（张逸凡摄影）
Flower Umbrella Dance (Three Umbrellas) (Photography by Zhang Yifan)

Naval Political Department and the Song and Dance Troupe of the Political Department of the PLA Air Force, successively came to Xinyang to learn this program. In 1959, the *Flower Umbrella Dance*, adapted from the dance "Six Umbrellas" was performed by the Central Song and Dance Troupe at the World Youth Festival in Vienna and won the silver medal. Now, the Flower Umbrella Dance has evolved into a pure dance, mainly in the form of group dance for girls.

三、农耕文明的音声场：民间戏剧

1. 掌上乾坤——皮影戏

淮河流域中上游地区有着浓郁的民间多神信仰气氛。其中，酬神还愿的传统习俗催生了本区域的仪式戏剧，而仪式戏剧的代表当属被称为掌上乾坤的戏剧形式皮影戏。

中国皮影戏共分河南、山西、陕西、唐山四大流派。淮河流域的皮影戏是河南皮影戏的代表之一，主要流传在豫南的桐柏县和信阳市，共有四百多个传统剧目，唱腔、道白、音乐、影人制作等都具有浓厚的地方特色。它综合了戏剧、音乐、美术等艺术门类，集文人写作、艺人刻绘与民间演唱为一体，蕴藏着极为丰富的文化内涵。

豫南皮影的影人水牛皮经过复杂工艺制成，其演出班社俗称"一担箱"，即所有道具只用两只小木箱就可全部盛下，每只箱子里都有三四百个不同的影人头和百八十个影人身，头和身可以根据演出剧目进行组合，山石草木、楼台亭宇、龙车凤辇、飞禽走兽，应有尽有，皇帝太监、文臣武将、神仙妖怪，一应俱全。

皮影戏班一般由五六个人组成，演出时就地搭台，挂一块宽6尺（2米）、高3尺（1米）的白布作影幕，白天用自然光源，夜晚用灯光照在幕布后面。每个影人由三根竹竿支撑（影人的脖子和双手各一根），演员操作三根小棍，使影人的形象映于影幕之上。根据剧情的发展，举、止、动、静，喜、怒、哀、乐的表现，都要靠演员拿影子的基本功。影子的拿法很有学问，讲究技巧，它需要根据剧中人物的行当不同而各有变化，即所谓的"影子戏好唱，三根棍难戳"。

豫南皮影戏的唱腔有东调与西调之分，唱腔音乐和当地山歌、地灯、花鼓戏有着密切的"血缘"关系，方言声调又渗透着湖广韵，形成了唱腔明亮、秀丽、委婉动听的特点。整体音乐由唱腔、唢呐或人声帮腔、

III. Sounds of Agricultural Civilization: Folk Operas

1. A Grand Stage in the Palm: Shadow Puppetry

In the middle and upper reaches of the Huaihe River Basin, there is a strong atmosphere of folk polytheistic belief. Among them, the traditional custom of rewarding the gods for fulfilling their wishes gives birth to the ritual opera in this region, and the representative of the ritual opera is the shadow puppetry, known as "a grand stage in the palm".

There are four schools of shadow puppetry in China: shadow puppetry of Henan, Shanxi, Shaanxi and Tangshan in Hebei Province. The shadow puppetry in the Huaihe River Basin is one branch of Henan shadow puppetry. It is mainly spread in Tongbai County and Xinyang City in southern Henan Province. There are more than 400 traditional plays with strong local characteristics, such as singing, acting, music and puppetry (with puppets made from buffalo hide). It involves drama, music, fine arts and other art categories, integrating writing, carving, painting, and folk singing.

The shadow puppetry troupe in southern Henan is commonly known as "a shoulder pole bearing two cases", that is, two small wooden cases are enough to hold all the items. In each box there are about 300–400 different puppetry heads and 80–100 bodies, which can be combined into different figures according to the performance.

The shadow puppetry troupe usually consists of five or six people. During the performance, they set up a stage on the spot and hang a white cloth about two meters wide and one meter high as a screen. They use natural light during the day and lamplight behind the screen at night. Each puppet is supported by three bamboo sticks (one for his neck and two for his hands), and the actor operates it with the three sticks. According to the plots, the delivery of the puppets' actions and emotions all depends on the basic skills of the actors. The manipulation of the puppet varies according to the character's profession in the play, that is to say, it is easy to tell the story in the shadow puppetry, but difficult to operate the three sticks.

Shadow puppetry in southern Henan can be divided into the eastern tune

打击乐三个部分组成。豫南皮影戏剧目丰富,据不完全调查,仅罗山县皮影戏经常上演的传统剧目就有 49 本 231 个,折子戏 167 个,现代戏 36 个。

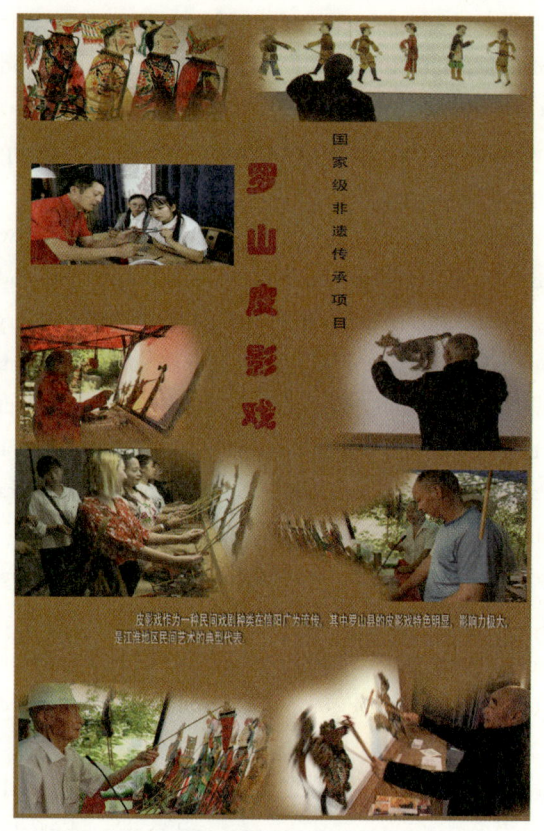

国家级非遗传承项目——罗山皮影戏(信阳学院冯春晓摄影)
National Intangible Cultural Heritage Project—Luoshan Shadow Puppetry (Photography by Feng Chunxiao, Xinyang University)

自 2008 年进入国家非物质文化遗产名录以来,豫南皮影戏越来越多地跨出地域局限,走向了更广阔的舞台。2018 年春节,应山西皇城相府景区邀请,豫南罗山皮影戏前往交流演出,连续演出 17 天 90 余场,观众达 4 万余人次。2017 年,罗山皮影戏新秀剧团应法国巴黎中国文化中心邀请,分别在巴黎中国文化中心和巴黎十三区政府,举办两场皮

and the western tune. The singing has a close "blood relationship" with the local mountain songs, ground lanterns and Huagu operas. The dialect tones also permeate the rhyme of Hubei and Hunan provinces. The whole music is composed of three parts: singing tune, *suona* or vocal accompaniment, and percussion music. There are abundant shadow puppetry pieces in southern Henan. According to an incomplete survey, in Luoshan County alone, there are 231 traditional pieces from 49 operas, 167 opera highlights and 36 modern operas.

Since its entry into the National Intangible Cultural Heritage List in 2008, shadow puppetry in southern Henan has stepped onto a broader stage. During the Spring Festival of 2018, at the invitation of House of the Huangcheng Chancellor scenic spot in Shanxi Province, Luoshan shadow puppetry in southern Henan performed more than 90 times in 17 days, attracting more than 40,000 audiences. In 2017, Luoshan shadow puppetry troupe, at the invitation of the Chinese Culture Center in Paris and the 13th Arrondissement of Paris, respectively held two shadow puppetry special performances, bringing the warmth and care of the motherland to the overseas Chinese, and spreading the traditional culture and art in the Huaihe River Basin to the world.

位于罗山县的皮影戏传承基地
Shadow Puppetry Inheriting Base in Luoshan County

影戏专场演出，豫南皮影戏的艺人们为华人华侨带去了祖国的温暖，将淮河流域传统文化艺术传播到了更广阔的世界。

2. 信阳民间戏剧"金名片"——光山花鼓戏

花鼓戏进课堂（信阳学院冯春晓摄影）
Huagu Opera in the Class（Photography by Feng Chunxiao, Xinyang University）

光山花鼓戏是流行于信阳一带的戏曲剧种，2014年入选国家非物质文化遗产名录。该剧种吸收了豫南地区汉族民间音乐并融合了楚剧、黄梅戏唱腔，拥有丰富的音乐语汇；道白使用方言、俚语，诙谐幽默；人员精干，一人多角，一唱众和；舞美，扮相简而不乱。

光山花鼓戏是光山县特有的民间艺术，清光绪年间，光山县已经有了杨堤盛花鼓戏班。薪火相传至今，光山花鼓戏从1967年以来多次赴北京人民大会堂演出，受到好评。由于种种原因，与其他民间艺术珍品一样，"花鼓戏"也面临着后继乏人、无法传承的窘境。为复兴这项民间艺术，政府超常规投入，先后募集资金300多万元，拯救"花鼓戏"。

2. "Golden Calling Card" of Xinyang Folk Operas—Guangshan Huagu Opera

Guangshan Huagu Opera is a kind of opera popular in Xinyang. It was listed as the National Intangible Cultural Heritage in 2014. This opera absorbs the folk music of Han people in southern Henan and integrates the singing tune of Chu Opera and Huangmei Opera, resulting in rich musical vocabulary. The dialogue or monologue uses humorous dialect and slang. In the opera, one person plays many roles, one person leads the singing and the others sing along; they dance beautifully, with simple costume and makeup, but incredibly orderly.

Guangshan Huagu Opera is a unique folk art in Guangshan County. During the reign of Emperor Guangxu of the Qing Dynasty (1875-1908), there was already Yang Disheng Huagu Opera Troupe in Guangshan County. Since 1967, Guangshan Huagu Opera has been performed in the Great Hall of the People in Beijing many times and has been well received. For a variety of reasons, Huagu Opera, like other folk arts, is also facing the dilemma of a lack of successors. In order to revive this folk art, the government has raised more than 3 million yuan

代表剧目《夫妻观灯》(信阳学院冯春晓摄影)
The Representative Repertory *Couples Watching the Lanterns* (Photography by Feng Chunxiao, Xinyang University)

如今,"光山花鼓戏"已有了 5 个培训基地,200 余名专兼职演员,来自医生、教师、农民等各行各业。"光山花鼓戏"已成为一张金名片。新版"花鼓戏"《夫妻观灯》《顶椅》等获全省地方剧目展演金奖,作为非遗项目经常出国交流演出。

现代花鼓戏《顶椅》(信阳学院冯春晓摄影)
Modern Huagu Opera *Carrying a Chair on the Head* (Photography by Feng Chunxiao, Xinyang University)

to rescue Huagu Opera. Now, there are five training bases for Guangshan Huagu Opera, with more than 200 full-time and part-time actors from all walks of life, including those with the professions of doctors, teachers and peasants. Guangshan Huagu Opera has become a calling card of Xinyang folk operas. The new versions of Huagu Opera, such as *Couples Watching the Lanterns* and *Carrying a Chair on the Head*, have won the gold medal of provincial local repertory performances. As intangible cultural heritage projects, the new versions of Guangshan Huagu Opera are often performed abroad.

第七章

典故篇：信阳典故

Chapter 7

Historic Tales: Historic Tales in Xinyang

信阳地处鄂豫皖三省交界，奔流不息的淮河见证了它的历史变迁。在中原文化、荆楚文化和吴越文化的影响下，它自成一体，形成了"豫风楚韵"的独特气质。信阳历史文化厚重，广为人知的三年不语息夫人、优孟衣冠、子路问津、亡羊补牢、司马光砸缸等历史典故和成语故事都发生在这里。信阳名人荟萃，有楚国令尹孙叔敖、战国四君子之一的春申君黄歇、蜀国贤臣费祎、名将魏延、"开漳圣王"陈元光、明代文坛领袖何景明等。信阳还是一座将星璀璨的革命红城，被誉为"红军的摇篮、将军的故乡"，成长出许世友、李德生、郑维山等近百名开国将军。关于他们的典故在民众中代代相传。

1. 三年不语息夫人

春秋时期诸侯众多，各自为政，互相攻伐兼并，中原一带更是扰攘不安。晋楚"城濮之战"以后，其余小国不是依晋，就是附楚，端赖强国的保护而生存，稍有不慎，随时都有玉石俱焚的灾祸降临。

息夫人息妫，是春秋时期陈国国君的女儿，后嫁给息国国君为妻。息夫人出嫁时路过蔡国，因姐妹嫁给蔡国国君蔡哀侯为妻，遂被留下见面，蔡哀侯对息夫人无礼。息侯听到此事大怒，于是派人请求楚国国君楚文王攻击蔡国。同年九月，楚军在莘地（今河南汝南县境）击败蔡军，俘虏蔡哀侯。然而，为了息国的生存，息夫人被迫侍奉楚王，并为楚王生了两个儿子。息夫人整日怀念故国，三年不语，从而留下了"三年不语息夫人"的典故。2021年，息夫人传说被列入第五批河南省非物质文化遗产代表性项目——民间文学名录。

Xinyang is located at the junction of Henan, Anhui and Hubei provinces. The ever-flowing Huaihe River has witnessed her historical vicissitude. Under the influence of the Central Plains culture, Jingchu culture and Wuyue culture, the culture in Xinyang has evolved in its own style, i.e., "a unique culture combining culture in Central China and culture in Chu Kingdom". Xinyang's culture has a long history and many well-known historic tales originated here, such as "Mrs. Xi Keeping Silent for Three Years", "The Actor Meng Dressing Up as Sunshu Ao", "Zi Lu Asking for the Ferry", "Locking the Barn Door After the Sheep Is Stolen", "Sima Guang Smashing the Vat", etc. There are also many celebrities here in Xinyang, including: Sunshu Ao, the prime minister in the Chu Kingdom; Huang Xie, Lord of Chunshen, one of the four lords during the Warring States Period; Fei Yi, the prime minister in the Shu Kingdom; Wei Yan, high-ranking military officer in the Han Dynasty; Chen Yuanguang, the Sacred Pioneer of Zhangzhou; and He Jingming, the literary leader in the Ming Dynasty, etc. Xinyang is also a revolutionary city, known as "the cradle for the Red Army" and "the hometown for generals". Nearly 100 generals upon whom the PRC was founded were born and grew here, such as Xu Shiyou, Li Desheng and Zheng Weishan, etc. And their miraculous stories have been passed down from generation to generation among people.

1. Mrs. Xi Keeping Silent for Three Years

In the Spring and Autumn Period, there were many feudal lords. They governed their own Kingdoms and fought each other, while the Central Plains was more seriously chaotic. After "the Battle of Chengpu" between Jin Kingdom and Chu Kingdom, other small states were either dependent on Jin Kingdom or Chu Kingdom for their survival, while any slightest mistakes might bring about disasters.

Xi Gui, the princess of Chen Kingdom in the Spring and Autumn Period, married the emperor of Xi Kingdom and was named as Mrs. Xi. On the way to marry, Mrs. Xi paid a visit to her sister in Cai Kingdom who was married to the emperor of Cai. While she was there, the emperor molested her. The emperor of Xi Kingdom got angry and asked for Chu's help. In September of the same year, the Chu's army fought against the Cai's army in Shen (present Runan County in

位于息州森林公园内的息夫人雕像（信阳学院冯葆炜摄影）

The Statue of Mrs. Xi in Xizhou Forest Park, Xi County（Photography by Feng Baowei, Xinyang University）

2. 优孟衣冠

春秋时期，楚国有位名字叫孟的优伶，因擅长幽默滑稽的乐舞戏谑而深得楚庄王的信任。优孟因演技精湛结识了许多朋友，其中就有令尹孙叔敖。

孙叔敖为官清廉，虽官位显赫，却无积蓄，他去世后，儿子生活非常艰难，靠砍柴为生。有一次他儿子去卖柴时遇见了优孟。优孟看到他贫穷困窘的模样感慨万分，回到家立即请裁缝按孙叔敖在世时常穿戴的衣物样式制作了一套衣冠，穿上后模仿他的音容笑貌。

不久楚庄王在宫中设宴庆祝寿诞，优孟扮作孙叔敖前去贺寿。酒席刚开始，扮作孙叔敖的优孟就立即上前祝福敬酒，楚庄王见后，以为孙叔敖死而复生，顿时大惊失色。当楚庄王知道那是优孟装扮的后，感慨万千，不由地想起孙叔敖辅佐他的那段岁月，他明白，如果没有孙叔敖

Henan Province) and captured the emperor of Cai Kingdom. For the survival of Xi Kingdom, Mrs. Xi was forced to be mistress of the emperor of Chu and bore him two sons. Heavily in homesickness, she kept silent for three years, which was passed down as a historic tale until now. In 2021, the historic tale was listed in the 5th batch of Henan Intangible Cultural Heritage—the catalogue of folk literature.

2. The Actor Meng Dressing Up as Sunshu Ao

In the Spring and Autumn Period, there was an opera actor named Meng who was skilled in funny and humorous dance and banter, and thus won the trust of Emperor Zhuang of Chu. Meng made many friends and one of them was Sunshu Ao, the prime minister in Chu Kingdom.

Sunshu Ao, though high in status, was an honest and upright official with little savings. When he passed away, his son lived a hard life by cutting firewood. Once when selling the firewood, he met actor Meng. Being frustrated at the situation of the son of Sunshu Ao, Meng immediately asked the tailor to make a dress which Sunshu Ao usually wore, and dressed it up to perform like what Sunshu Ao usually looked like.

Soon the Emperor Zhuang of Chu held a banquet for his birthday, and Meng dressed up as Sunshu Ao to celebrate his birthday. When Meng toasted to the emperor, he was startled and took it for granted that Sunshu Ao came back to life. When it turned out to be Meng in disguise, Emperor Zhuang was emotional and couldn't help remembering how Sunshu Ao had assisted him in governing the kingdom. He realized that without Sunshu Ao's help to tame the flood, he couldn't have achieved so much.

So, the Emperor Zhuang appointed Meng as the prime minister, but Meng refused. The emperor insisted, and then Meng responded that he would consult with his wife and reply after three days. Three days later, the actor Meng told the emperor that his wife didn't agree because Sunshu Ao was honest and upright to make the Chu Kingdom become a powerful state, but his son lived a hard life after his death. Meng would rather commit suicide than accept the emperor's proposal. Meng cried while he said this. The emperor felt very sorry and was moved to tears when he recalled Sunshu Ao's contributions.

The following day, the emperor summoned Sunshu Ao's son and appointed

治水，就没有楚国的今天。

爱屋及乌，楚庄王要任命优孟为令尹，优孟回绝，但是楚庄王执意要任命优孟为令尹。优孟回答说要回去与夫人商量，三日之后答复他。三天之后，优孟回复说夫人不让他到朝廷去当官，因为当年孙叔敖公正廉洁，帮助楚王称霸天下，死后，他的儿子却无立锥之地，如果真要像孙叔敖那样做令尹，还不如自杀算了。优孟说着说着，也是泪流满面，楚庄王回想起孙叔敖的功绩，十分愧疚，也不禁潸然泪下。

第二天，楚庄王便召见了孙叔敖的儿子，让他在朝中或富饶之地任职，被拒绝了。楚庄王问他有什么要求，他按父亲生前的嘱咐说："大王如果真的怜恤小民，就请将寝丘那片贫瘠之地赏赐给我吧，这样我们全家就可以生活了。"楚庄王当即下令，把寝丘的城邑封给他。从此之后，孙叔敖的子孙就从困境中解脱出来了。

3. 子路问津

"子路问津"的典故发生在信阳市罗山县。明、清两代曾设立三块"子路问津处"石碑。公元前497年，55岁的孔子离开鲁国，开始周游列国。公元前489年，孔子在陈蔡绝粮被困七日之后前往楚国负函（今信阳平桥区长台关乡城阳城一带），途中，眼看目的地就要到了，可是前面有一条河流挡住了去路却找不到渡口。正当一筹莫展之时，大家看到两位老人正在低头锄地。这两位老人正是当时隐居在这里的高士长沮和桀溺。孔子派大弟子子路前去向两位隐士请教渡口的位置。然而，隐士在讲述一番道理后，并没有告诉他渡口的位置。子路悻悻而归，把长沮和桀溺两位隐士的话转述给老师。

孔子听后若有所失地告诉他的弟子："人是不能同飞鸟走兽为伍的。鸟是飞的，在天空中可以自由飞翔；兽是山林中的，可以无忧无虑地行走。人各有志，只有各走各的路好了。可是，我们不同世上的人打交道，还同谁打交道呢？如果天下太平，符合正道，我也没有必要这么辛苦周

him an official position either in the court or in some lands of plenty, but his son refused. Then the emperor asked him what he wanted. He said as his father's will, "If your Majesty took pity on me, please give Qinqiu, the barren area, as a reward to me, and so, we can live on it." The emperor immediately gave an order to grant him cities and towns around Qinqiu. From then on, the offsprings of Sunshu Ao were freed from the predicament.

3. Zi Lu Asking for the Ferry

This historic tale happened in Luoshan County, Xinyang, where three stone tablets were set up respectively in the Ming and Qing dynasties with the inscription of "Zi Lu Asking for the Ferry". In 497 BC, Confucius and his disciples left Lu Kingdom and started their journey around the Kingdoms. In 489 BC, they went for Fuhan (persent Chengyangcheng, Changtaiguan Town, Pingqiao District, Xinyang) in Chu Kingdom after being trapped in Chen and Cai Kingdoms without any food for seven days. On the way, when the destination was in sight, there was a river blocking the way and they couldn't find the ferry. When they had no idea to tackle with the problem, they saw two old farmers hoeing in the field. The two were Changju and Jieni, the learned men living here in seclusion. Confucius sent his disciple Zi Lu to ask them for the location of the

位于罗山的"子路问津处"石碑（信阳学院冯春晓摄影）
The Stone Tablet of "Zi Lu Asking for the Ferry" Located in Luoshan County (Photography by Feng Chunxiao, Xinyang University)

游列国力图改变这个乱世了！"后来，在一位农夫的指点下，孔子和他的弟子在太阳快要落山的时候终于找到了渡口，过了河，并顺利到达负函。这便是子路问津的典故。

4. 亡羊补牢

亡羊补牢的典故载自《战国策》："见兔而顾犬，未为晚也；亡羊而补牢，未为迟也。"公元前 278 年，秦国名将白起率军攻占楚国都城郢（今湖北江陵西北），楚顷襄王带着楚国的王公贵族逃亡到了城阳城（今信阳平桥区城阳城和长台关乡一带），以此作为楚国的陪都。此后，楚顷襄王非常懊悔当初没有听从谋臣庄辛的劝告，于是派人请回庄辛，寻求治国安邦良策，这便有了《战国策》"庄辛说楚顷襄王"的千古美谈。在庄辛的大力扶助下，楚顷襄王采用"见兔顾犬""亡羊补牢"的计策，凭借义阳三关和淮河天险，用"申、息之师"，很快渡过了危机，扭转了局势，收复了淮河以北大片失地，继而迁都于陈（今河南淮阳），使楚国历史又延续了 55 年。河南信阳一带在战国末期一度成为楚国的大本营和复兴基地。

5. 春申君黄歇

春申君黄歇是江南一带人文始祖，他游学博闻，善辩，楚考烈王元年为相，赐其淮河以北十二县，封为春申君，与魏国信陵君魏无忌、赵国平原君赵胜、齐国孟尝君田文并称为"战国四公子"。公元前 238 年，楚考烈王病逝，黄歇前去奔丧，李园令人埋伏于棘门之内，杀死春申君及其全家。

楚王因他游学博闻、能言善辩，于公元前 273 年派其到秦国议和。黄歇以当时联楚与攻楚的实际厉害关系说服了秦王，并派使者与秦签订了和约，使楚在千钧一发的情况下能够转危为安。

ferry, however, the hermits, after some argumentation, did not tell him where the ferry was. Zi Lu returned disappointedly and told Confucius what they said.

Confucius said to his disciples with a vague sense of loss, "Humans are different from birds or animals. Birds can fly in the sky without any constraint and animals can wend their way around in the forest without any fear. On the contrary, every person has his own ambition, and thus, different people have different pursuits. If we didn't make contact with other people, who else could we make contact with? If the world was at peace, it wouldn't necessary for us to make every effort to travel around all the kingdoms and change the current situation of the world." Later, they spotted the ferry at sunset with the help of a farmer, crossed the river and reached Fuhan. This is the historic tale—"Zi Lu Asking for the Ferry".

4. Locking the Barn Door After the Sheep Is Stolen

This historic tale is from *Strategies of the Warring States*, "It is not too late to call the dog after seeing the rabbit; it is also not too late to lock the barn door after the horse is stolen." In 278 BC, the famous general Bai Qi in the Qin Kingdom attacked the capital Ying of the Chu Kingdom (present northwest of Jiangling, Hubei Province) with his army. The Emperor Qingxiang of Chu fled away to the Chengyang City (present Chengyangcheng and Changtaiguan Town in Xinyang), which became the provisional capital of the Chu Kingdom. From then on, the Emperor Qingxiang felt so regretful that he hadn't accepted Zhuangxin's advice, and thus, he sent his counselor to invite Zhuangxin back and explored the strategies to govern his new Kingdom and ensure its security. This made the story "Zhuangxin persuaded the Emperor Qingxiang in the Chu Kingdom" come down in *Strategies of the Warring States*. With the help of Zhuangxin, the Emperor Qingxiang took the strategy of "locking the barn door after the horse is stolen", surviving the crisis by virtue of local geographical advantage, reversed the current situation and recovered the northern areas of the Huaihe River. Subsequently, he moved the capital to Chen (present Huaiyang County, Henan Province) and Chu Kingdom continued to last for 55 years. Xinyang has ever been camp and base for Chu's revitalization to the later period of the Warring States Period.

战国四公子之一春申君（信阳学院冯春晓摄影）
Lord of Chunshen—One of the Four Lords During the Warring States Period
(Photography by Feng Chunxiao, Xinyang University)

6. 司马光砸缸

司马光是北宋著名的文学家、史学家、政治家，生于信阳光山，世称涑水先生，编纂了中国第一部编年体通史《资治通鉴》，有"砸缸"的美谈传于世间。据传，有一次，司马光跟小伙伴们在县衙后院（现司马光宾馆）玩耍，有个小孩爬到大缸上玩，失足掉到缸里的水中。别的孩子一见出了事，都惊慌失措跑去，司马光却急中生智，从地上捡起一块大石头，使劲向水缸击去，水涌出来，小孩也得救了。此时，司马光也仅仅是一个七岁的孩子。人们知道后，纷纷称赞司马光的勇敢行为，为他的机智点赞。这就是著名的"司马光砸缸"的典故。

5. The Lord of Chunshen—Huang Xie

Huang Xie, the Lord of Chunshen, is known as first ancestor of civilization in the south of the Yangtze River. He travelled a lot, learned and eloquent. He was appointed as the prime minister in the first year that Emperor Kaolie of the Chu Kingdom was in power. Huang Xie was then awarded 12 counties in the north of the Huaihe River and called Lord of Chunshen. Together with Wei Wuji, the Lord of Xinling in the Wei Kingdom, Zhao Sheng, the Lord of Pingyuan in the Zhao Kingdom, and Tian Wen, the Lord of Mengchang in the Qi Kingdom, Huang Xie was known as one of the four lords during the Warring States Period. In 238 BC, the Emperor Kaolie died of disease and Huang Xie went to the funeral. Li Yuan asked his soldiers to ambush in Jimen. Huang Xie and his family were all killed.

Due to Huang Xie's eloquence and erudition, the emperor of the Chu Kingdom sent him to make peace with the emperor of the Qin Kingdom in 273 BC. Huang Xie persuaded the emperor of the Qin Kingdom by telling him the possible consequence of the alliance with the Chu Kingdom or the attack to the Chu Kingdom. Finally, he made agreement with the Qin Kingdom and the Chu Kingdom was finally out of danger.

6. Sima Guang Smashing the Vat

Sima Guang was a famous litterateur, historian, and statesman in the Northern Song Dynasty. Born in Guangshan County, Xinyang, generally known as Mr. Sushui, he compiled *Zizhitongjian*, the first general history in annalistic style in China, and was prestigious for the historic tale "Sima Guang Smashing the Vat". It is said that when Sima Guang was playing with his kid friends in the backyard of the County Administrative Building (present Sima Guang Hotel), there was one playing on the edge of the huge vat and falling accidentally into it. When the others were all panic-stricken and ran away, Sima Guang kept calm, picked up a stone and smashed the vat broken, and the child survived. At that time, Sima Guang was only 7 years old. When people heard this, they all praised his bravery and intelligence. This is the well-known historic tale—"Sima Guang Smashing the Vat".

光山司马光故居"司马光砸缸"雕塑（信阳学院冯春晓摄影）
The Statue of "Sima Guang Smashing the Vat" in the Former Residence of Sima Guang, Guangshan County（Photography by Feng Chunxiao, Xinyang University）

7. 何景明

何景明是明代"文坛四杰"中的重要人物，也是明代著名的"前七子"之一，与李梦阳并称文坛领袖。何景明一生为人耿直，凡是权贵不交，宦官不交，从任上病归时，只有白银30两。

何景明作为皇帝的钦差大臣出使滇南归来，不取地方官吏贡献一金一物。他看到宦官刘瑾擅权、贪赃枉法，敢于直言纳束，上书吏部尚书，劝其秉政毋挠。当文坛挚友李梦阳受迫害被关到江西牢狱时，人人自危，唯何景明上书吏部为之奔呼，并在《应诏陈言治安疏》里，揭露皇帝存在的四个错误：义子不当蓄，边军不当留，番僧不当宠，宦官不当任。

8. 许世友将军

上将许世友，1905年出生于河南省信阳市新县田铺乡河铺村许家洼。由于家境贫寒，他8岁便随拳师入少林寺，在少林寺做了8年苦役，亦

7. He Jingming

He Jingming was one of the Four Literary Celebrities and also one of the Former Seven Litterateurs of the Ming Dynasty. He Jingming and Li Mengyang were considered as the two leading figures in literary field at that time. He was notably honest and upright, neither making friends with bigwigs, nor with eunuchs, and when he retired from the official position because of illness, there were only 30 *liang* silver ingots left (roughly equivalent to 6,000 *yuan* at present).

When He Jingming was appointed as Imperial Commissioner to inspect the south of Yunnan Province, he didn't take anything from local officials. When he saw the eunuch Liu Jin aggregate all powers to himself and take bribes, he dared to speak bluntly to the emperor and demanded that the minister of Official Personnel Affairs adhere to the administrative regulations. When his best friend Li Mengyang was persecuted and put into prison, every official felt insecure, but only He Jingming tried to save him. In the article *The Proposal of Public Security According to Imperial Decree*, he revealed the emperor's four mistakes: the emperor should not adopt sons; frontier soldiers shouldn't stay at the capital city; monks from the Western Regions shouldn't be the emperor's favorites; eunuchs shouldn't be in official positions.

8. General Xu Shiyou

General Xu Shiyou was born in 1905 in Hepu Village, Xinxian County, Xinyang City. Due to the poor family, he went to Shaolin Temple with the boxer at the age of 8, and did 8 years of hard labor there, but as well mastered the super Shaolin Kung Fu. His Shaolin Kung Fu served him during his whole revolutionary career. In the Red Army, he was successively appointed as the head of Dare-to-Die Corps 6 times, even after when he was already an army commander. And he has also been wounded for 8 times in the battle field. In 1955, General Xu Shiyou was honored with the land admiral rank.

General Xu Shiyou was a well-known filial son to his parents. He felt very regretful that he couldn't look after his mother in several decades of revolutionary life. When he was appointed as a commander in Shandong military region in 1952, he applied for home leave once. When face to face with his mother, he knelt down before his mother and was reluctant to stand up only after the neighbouring

练就一身硬功夫。他的一身武艺在革命生涯中发挥了神奇作用。在红军中，他当过6次敢死队队长，8次负伤，甚至在当了军长后还担任过敢死队队长。1955年许世友将军被授予上将军衔。

许世友将军是远近闻名的大孝子，然而参加革命队伍以后，几十年戎马倥偬，为国尽忠，顾不上对母亲尽孝，内心常存歉疚之情。1952年任山东军区司令员时，他曾请假探家一次，见了母亲，长跪不起，众人百般劝慰才把他扶起来。1959年，为看地形他又一次路过家门，见74岁的老母亲还在打柴、喂猪，不禁泪流满面。母亲病危时，他因公务缠身，未及赶回去给老人送终，引为终生憾事。当时他发下誓愿：自己死后，一定来为母亲守坟。缘于这笔"感情债"，许世友才没有在中央关于领导工作人员实行火葬的"倡议书"上签名。1985年10月22日，许世友病逝，终于完成了自己"活着尽忠，死后尽孝"的誓愿，魂归故里，守在母亲身边。

在长期的文明发展中，信阳累积了很多广为流传的典故，这些典故滋养着一代又一代人，逐渐成为信阳的文化符号。这些典故的传播，对传承、弘扬中华优秀传统美德都具有重要的价值和意义。

villagers had made painstaking effort to persuade him. In 1959, he passed through his hometown again to check the local geography, and when he saw his 74-year-old mother still doing farm work, his face was covered with tears. It was a lifelong regret for him that he couldn't come home because of official business when his mother was at death's door. At that time, he swore that he would stay with his mother after he passed away. Because of this emotional guilt, he didn't sign his name on the written proposal issued by Party Central Committee for the leaders and government staff implementing cremation. General Xu Shiyou passed away on October 22, 1985 and was buried beside his mother's grave, fulfilling his goal of "serving his country in life, paying filial piety after death".

With the long-term development of civilization, there were many historic tales accumulated in Xinyang. Passed on from one generation to the next and gradually, the unique culture of Xinyang came into being. The propagation of these historic tales is of significance in advocating traditional Chinese virtues.

第八章

前景篇：淮河与"一带一路"

Chapter 8

Prospects: The Huaihe River and the Belt and

Road Initiative

一、国家战略：淮河生态经济带

淮河流域地处长江流域和黄河流域之间，经济发展总体相对滞后，是我国中东部最具发展潜力的地区之一。2018年10月6日，国务院批复同意《淮河生态经济带发展规划》，这标志着首个跨省域的生态经济带发展规划正式上升为国家战略，为淮河流域带来了千载难逢的发展"东风"。

在中国特色社会主义进入新时代和生态文明建设不断向纵深推进的大背景下，加快淮河生态经济带发展，对于推进生态文明建设、促进经济社会持续健康发展、推动区域协调发展、全面建成小康社会具有重要意义；有利于推动淮河全流域综合治理，打好流域污染防治攻坚战，探索大河流域生态文明建设新模式；有利于打造我国新的出海水道，全面融入"一带一路"建设，打造中东部地区开放发展新的战略支点，完善我国对外开放新格局；有利于推进产业转型升级和新旧动能转换，确保国家粮食安全，培育我国经济发展新支撑带；有利于优化城镇格局，发挥优势推动中部地区崛起和东部地区优化发展，打赢精准脱贫攻坚战，推动形成区域协调发展新局面。

1. 发展基础

淮河生态经济带以淮河干流、一级支流以及下游沂沭泗水系流经的地区为规划范围，包括河南、湖北、安徽、山东、江苏5省25个地市和4个县(市)，其中涉及河南的信阳市、驻马店市、周口市、漯河市、商丘市、平顶山市和南阳市桐柏县，规划面积24.3万平方公里，2017年末常住人口1.46亿，地区生产总值6.75万亿元。

（1）区位条件优越

淮河生态经济带贯通黄淮平原，连接中东部，通江达海，与长江经济带地域相连、水系相通，京沪、京九、京广、陇海等国家主干铁路和长深、

I. National Strategy: The Ecological Economic Belt Along the Huaihe River

Located between the Yangtze River Basin and the Yellow River Basin, the overall economic development of the Huaihe River Basin is considerably lagging behind, hence it is one of the regions with great potentials in Central and East China. On October 6th, 2018, the State Council approved *The Development Planning for Ecological Economic Belt Along the Huaihe River*, which symbolizes that the first trans-provincial ecological economic belt development planning has been formally upgraded to national strategy and accelerates the development along the Huaihe River.

With the entering of the new era of Socialism with Chinese Characteristics, and under the background of further promotion of ecological civilization construction, accelerating the development of ecological economic belt along the Huaihe River is of great significance in impelling the ecological civilization construction, promoting the sustainable and healthy development of economy and society, facilitating coordinated development between regions, and building a moderately prosperous society in all respects. It is conducive to promoting the comprehensive management of the Huaihe River Basin, fighting for pollution prevention and control along the Huaihe River, and exploring a new mode of ecological civilization construction along the basin of large rivers. To accelerate the development of ecological economic belt along the Huaihe River could also help to build a new waterway toward the sea in China, fully integrate the basin into the Belt and Road Initiative, create a new strategic fulcrum for the opening up and development of the central and eastern China, and improve the new pattern of China's opening up. Additionally, it may help in promoting the industrial transformation and upgrading, transforming energy supplies from old patterns to new patterns, ensuring national food security, and developing the new zone for Chinese economic development. Finally, it will help to optimize the urban structure, promote the rise of the central region and the optimized development of the eastern region, win the battle of targeted poverty alleviation and make new progress in the coordinated development among regions.

美丽的淮河（信阳学院冯葆炜摄影）
The Beautiful Huaihe River (Photography by Feng Baowei, Xinyang University)

沈海等高速公路在此交汇，淮河水系通航里程约2300公里，京杭大运河、淮河干流及主要支流航运较为发达。

（2）自然禀赋优良

该区域位于我国南北气候过渡带，生物多样性丰富，平原面积广阔，生态系统较为稳定，是我国重要的商品粮基地和棉花、油料、水果、蔬菜等重要产区，湖泊众多，水系发达，水产养殖业和畜牧业潜力巨大，矿产资源储量丰富、品种繁多，是华东地区重要的煤炭和能源基地。

（3）发展潜力巨大

人力资源丰富，城镇化和消费市场潜力大。产业体系较为完备，装备制造、有色金属、食品加工等产业集群优势明显，高技术产业和战略性新兴产业发展迅速。毗邻长江三角洲等经济发达地区，承接产业转移的基础条件较好。

1. Development Foundation

The ecological economic belt along the Huaihe River covers the areas of the main stream of the Huaihe River, its primary tributary and the Yi-Shu-Si River system, including 25 cities and 4 counties in the five provinces of Henan, Hubei, Anhui, Shandong, and Jiangsu. The planned area in Henan Province is 243,000 square kilometers, including Xinyang, Zhumadian, Zhoukou, Luohe, Shangqiu, Pingdingshan and Tongbai County in Nanyang. At the end of 2017, the population of permanent residents was 146 million and the gross regional product amounts to 6.75 trillion *yuan* in the planned area.

千里长淮万卷书，四季浪花唱古今（信阳学院冯葆炜摄影）
The Huaihe River, a Thousand Miles, Runs Endlessly Eastward,
Story in Volumes, Past and Present, Witnesses the Chinese Vicissitude (Photography by Feng Baowei, Xinyang University)

(1) Favorable Location

The ecological economic belt along the Huaihe River runs through the plain between the Yellow River and the Huaihe River, connecting the central and eastern China and is accessible to different rivers and seas of the country. It is geographically adjacent to the economic belt along the Yangtze River both in land and water. The national trunk railways and expressways such as Beijing-Shanghai, Beijing-Kowloon, Beijing-Guangzhou, Lanzhou-Lianyungang railways and Changchun-Shenzhen and Shenyang-Haikou highways meet here. There are about 2,300 kilometers of navigable waterway along the Huaihe River, and the Beijing-Hangzhou Grand Canal, the Huaihe trunk stream and its main tributaries are well developed.

南湾湖开渔时节（桂莹玉摄影）
Fishing Season in the Nanwan Lake (Photography by Gui Yingyu)

（4）文化底蕴深厚

淮河流域是中华文明的重要发祥地，拥有楚汉文化、红色文化、大运河文化等丰富多彩的文化资源，国家历史文化名城、全国重点文物保护单位数量众多，群众性文化活动丰富，为在新时代弘扬中华优秀传统文化、推动文化事业和文化产业发展奠定了良好基础。

2. 战略定位

（1）流域生态文明建设示范带

把生态保护和环境治理放在首要位置，建立健全跨区域生态建设和

(2) Favorable Natural Resources

Because the ecological economic belt along the Huaihe River is located in the transitional zone from north to south climate, there is a vast plain area with biological diversity and comparatively stable ecosystem. It is an important grain production base and a major production area for cotton, oil crops, fruits, vegetables, etc. Due to abundant water resources, there is great potential for aquaculture and animal husbandry. Due to abundant reserve and diversity in mineral resources, it is the most important coal and energy base in eastern China.

(3) Great Development Potential

There are abundant human resources, great possibility of urbanization and great potential for consumer market. The industrial system is comparatively integrated. There are clear advantages in equipment manufacturing, non-ferrous metal industry, food processing industry, etc., and rapid developments in high-tech and emerging industries suitable for national strategy. Adjacent to the developed Yangtze River Delta, the ecological economic belt along the Huaihe River has great potential for industrial transportation.

(4) Profound Cultural Deposits

The Huaihe River Basin is the important cradle of Chinese civilization, including such various cultural resources as the Chu-Han culture(culture of the Chu and Han kingdoms), the Revolutionary culture and the Grand Canal culture, etc. There are a large number of state-level historic and cultural cities and key cultural relics under national protection. The diversity of mass cultural activities lays a good foundation for carrying forward Chinese traditional culture and promoting the development of public cultural undertakings and industries.

2. Strategic Positioning

(1) The Ecological Civilization Construction Exemplary Belt Along the Huaihe River Basin

The construction of the belt should give priority to ecological protection and environmental management. A trans-regional cooperation system should be formulated to coordinate the development, construction and environmental protection in the upper, middle and lower reaches of the Huaihe River Basin. And the strictest regulations of water resource management and environmental

环境保护的联动机制，统筹上中下游开发建设与生态环境保护，落实最严格的水资源管理制度和环境保护制度，着力保护水资源和水环境，加强流域综合治理和森林湿地保护修复，加快形成绿色发展方式和生活方式，把淮河流域建设成为天蓝地绿水清、人与自然和谐共生的绿色发展带，为全国大河流域生态文明建设积累新经验、探索新路径。

（2）特色产业创新发展带

加快实施创新驱动发展战略，加强分工协作，联手推进科技创新，着力培育新技术、新产业、新业态、新模式，推动产业跨界融合发展，加快传统产业转型升级，壮大提升战略性新兴产业，培育一批先进制造业龙头企业和优势产业集群，巩固提升全国重要粮食生产基地的地位，探索推进资源枯竭城市、老工业基地转型升级的有效途径，促进新旧动能转换和产业转型升级。

（3）新型城镇化示范带

构建大中小城市和小城镇协调发展的城镇格局，增强区域中心城市综合实力，促进大中小城市、特色小镇和美丽乡村协调发展，积极推进新型城镇化综合试点，分类引导农业转移人口市民化，实现产、城、人、文融合发展，完善城镇基础设施，增强公共服务供给能力，推进城乡基本公共服务一体化，全面提高城镇化水平和质量，努力在宜居宜业、城乡统筹发展方面探索新模式、新路径。

（4）中东部合作发展先行区

立足上中下游区域比较优势，发挥淮河水道和新亚欧大陆桥经济走廊纽带作用，促进基础设施对接、合作平台共建、基本公共服务共享，全面深化区域合作交流，引导资金技术向内陆腹地转移，营造与国内外市场接轨的制度环境，加快构建全方位、多层次、宽领域的开放合作新格局，形成联动中东部、协调南北方的开放型经济带。

protection should also be fully implemented to protect the water resource and water environment. It is supposed to reinforce the integrated management and the restoration of forest wetland to accelerate the formation of new types of development pattern (well-balanced between economic development and environmental protection) and green development way and lifestyle, so as to build up a green development zone with blue sky, clear water and harmonious mankind and nature relationship in the Huaihe River Basin, and accumulate new experience and explore new paths for ecological progress in major river basins across the country.

(2) The Distinctive Industry Innovation and Development Belt

It is necessary to accelerate the implementation of innovation-driven development strategy, to strengthen cooperation, to promote scientific and technological innovation and to cultivate new technology, new industry, new form of industry and new models. It is important to promote cross-industry integrated development, to accelerate the transformation and upgrading of traditional industries, to promote the emerging industries suitable for national strategy, and to foster a number of leading enterprises in advanced manufacturing and advantageous industrial clusters. It is supposed to consolidate and upgrade its status as a national vital grain production base, to explore the effective ways of transformation and upgrading of resource-exhausted cities and traditional industrial base and to promote the transformation of the kinesthetic energy from the old to the new pattern and the transformation and upgrading of industries.

(3) The New Pattern Urbanization Exemplary Belt

Constructing a pattern of coordinated development between cities and small towns may reinforce the comprehensive strength of the central cities in the region and promote the coordinated development of large, medium and small cities, small towns with distinctive features, and beautiful villages. It is supposed to actively carry out comprehensive trials of a new type of urbanization, provide classified guidance for the citizenization of rural migrants, achieve integrated development of industry, urban areas, residents and culture, improve urban infrastructure, enhance the ability to supply public services, promote the integration of urban and rural basic public services, and finally comprehensively raise the level and quality of urbanization. It is necessary to spare no efforts to explore new models and new

3. 空间布局

根据主体功能分区，优化生态安全屏障体系，坚持以资源环境承载能力为基础，发挥各地比较优势，促进沿淮集聚发展、流域互动协作，明确空间开发重点和方向，构建"一带、三区、四轴、多点"的总体格局。

"一带"：指淮河干流绿色发展带。加强淮河干流及沿线地区生态系统保护和修复，提升生态系统质量和稳定性，构筑具有防洪、水土保持、水源涵养等复合功能的沿淮综合植被防护体系。充分发挥淮河干流水道作用，加快推进淮河出海航道建设和中下游航道疏浚，增强干流航运能力，大力发展多式联运，加快沿淮铁路、高速公路和集疏运体系建设，合理推进岸线开发和港口建设，构建综合立体交通走廊。增强信阳、徐州、淮安、盐城、阜阳、蚌埠辐射带动能力，建立健全绿色低碳循环发展的经济体系，推进资源全面节约和循环利用，形成特色鲜明、布局合理、生态良好的现代特色产业和城镇密集带。

"三区"：指东部海江河湖联动区、北部淮海经济区、中西部内陆崛起区。东部海江河湖联动区包括淮安、盐城、扬州、泰州、滁州等市，

位于中西部内陆崛起区的河南信阳市（信阳学院冯春晓摄影）

Xinyang, Henan Province, Located in the Inland Revivification Zone in Mid-west China
(Photography by Feng Chunxiao, Xinyang University)

paths for better living and working conditions and balanced development between urban and rural areas.

(4) Central and Eastern China Cooperation Development Pilot Zone

The relatively different advantages of the upper, middle and lower reaches of the Huaihe River Basin can trigger the combination between waterways in the Huaihe River and the economic development along the New Asian-European Land Bridge; promote infrastructure connectivity, build cooperation platforms, and share basic public services. At the same time, it is important to comprehensively deepen trans-regional cooperation and communication, to transfer technology and finance to inland cities, and to create an institutional environment that is in line with domestic and foreign markets. What's more, it must accelerate the step of building a new pattern of all-dimensional, multi-tiered and wide-ranging opening up and cooperation, and form an open economic belt that links the central and eastern regions and coordinates the south and the north.

3. Space Layout

Based on the optimisation of ecological security and the degree of utilizing natural resources, it is necessary to release potential advantages in different areas to push ahead with the development along the Huaihe River and the cooperation between the Huaihe River Basin, and to clarify the key issue and the orientation of future geographic exploitation, and to construct the overall pattern of "One Belt, Three Districts, Four Axes, Multiple Sites".

"One Belt" refers to the Huaihe River Main Stream Green Development Belt. It is significant to reinforce the ecological protection and restoration along the main stream of the Huaihe River, improve the quality and stability of the ecosystem, and build a comprehensive vegetation protection system along the Huaihe River with multiple functions such as flood control, and soil and water conservation. As for the transportation, it is of vital importance to make full use of the function of the trunk stream waterway, speed up the construction of the main waterway to the sea and the dredging of the middle and lower reaches of the Huaihe River, enhance the shipping capacity of the main waterway, vigorously develop multimodal transport, speed up the construction of railways, expressways and the distribution system along the Huaihe River, rationally promote the

发挥淮安、盐城区域中心城市的引领作用,依托洪泽湖、高邮湖、南四湖等重要湖泊水体,统筹海江河湖生态文明建设,强化与长江三角洲、皖江城市带等周边区域对接互动。北部淮海经济区包括徐州、连云港、宿迁、宿州、淮北、商丘、枣庄、济宁、临沂、菏泽等市,着力提升徐州区域中心城市辐射带动能力,发挥连云港新亚欧大陆桥经济走廊东方起点和陆海交汇枢纽作用,推动淮海经济区协同发展。中西部内陆崛起区包括信阳、驻马店、周口、漯河、平顶山、桐柏、蚌埠、淮南、阜阳、六安、亳州、随县、广水、大悟等市(县),发挥信阳、蚌埠、阜阳区域中心城市的辐射带动作用,积极承接产业转移,推动资源型城市转型发展,因地制宜发展生态经济,加快新型城镇化和农业现代化进程。

"四轴":依托新(沂)长(兴)铁路、京沪高速公路、京杭运河以及在建的连淮扬镇高铁、规划建设的京沪高铁二通道,建设临沂—连云港—宿迁—淮安—盐城—扬州—泰州发展轴;依托京广线,建设漯河—驻马店—信阳发展轴;依托京九线,建设菏泽—商丘—亳州—阜阳—六安发展轴;依托京沪铁路与高铁,建设济宁—枣庄—徐州—淮北—宿州—蚌埠—淮南—滁州发展轴。依托四条发展轴,向南对接长三角城市群、长江中游城市群、皖江城市带,向北对接京津冀地区、中原城市群,着力吸引人口、产业聚集,辐射带动苏北、皖北、豫东、鲁南、鄂东北等区域发展。

"多点":指区域中心城市之外的其他城市。壮大城市规模和综合实力,完善城市功能,因地制宜发展特色优势产业,提升基础设施和公共服务供给能力,吸引农业转移人口加快集聚,加强与区域中心城市的经济联系与互动,发挥对淮河生态经济带发展的多点支撑作用,增强对周边地区发展的辐射带动能力。

development of the shoreline and the port construction, and finally build a comprehensive and three-dimensional transportation corridor. What's more, it is necessary to enhance the radiation driving capacity of Xinyang, Xuzhou, Huai'an, Yancheng, Fuyang and Bengbu, establish and improve the economic system of green, low-carbon and circular development, promote the comprehensive conservation and recycling of resources, and finally establish a modern featured industry and dense distributed city belts with distinctive features, reasonable layout and friendly ecology.

"Three Districts" refer to the River, Lake and Sea Linkage Zone in east of China, the Huaihai Economic Zone in the north of China, the Inland Revivification Zone in the mid-west of China. In the east of China, the River, Lake and Sea Linkage Zone includes cities like Huai'an, Yancheng, Yangzhou, Taizhou and Chuzhou, etc. Taking advantage of the leading role played by the central regional cities such as Huai'an and Yancheng, it is necessary to make overall plans for the ecologically conscious construction of water resources based on important lakes such as the Hongze Lake, Gaoyou Lake and Nansi Lake, and at the same time strengthen the communication of the zone with the Yangtze River Delta and perimeter zones of cities in Anhui and Jiangxi provinces. In the north of China, the Huaihai Economic Zone includes the cities such as Xuzhou, Lianyungang, Suqian, Suzhou, Huaibei, Shangqiu, Zaozhuang, Jining, Linyi and Heze, etc. Efforts should be made to enhance the radiation driving capacity of Xuzhou as a regional central city, and it is also necessary to attach great importance to the role of Lianyungang as the eastern starting point of New Eurasian Land Bridge Economic Corridor and land-sea intersection hub so as to promote the coordinated development of the Huaihai Economic Zone. In mid-west China, the Inland Revivification Zone includes the cities of Xinyang, Zhumadian, Zhoukou, Luohe, Pingdingshan, Tongbai, Bengbu, Huainan, Fuyang, Liu'an, Bozhou, Suixian, Guangshui, and Dawu. With the leading role of Xinyang, Bengbu and Fuyang, it is necessary to transfer some industries, to promote the transformation and development of resource-based cities, to develop the ecological economy according to local conditions and finally to accelerate the urbanization and the modernization of agriculture.

"Four Axes" refer to the development axis from Linyi to Taizhou, passing

信阳羊山新区百花园夜景（信阳学院冯葆炜摄影）
The Night View of Baihua Square in Yangshan New District, Xinyang (Photography by Feng Baowei, Xinyang University)

4. 发展目标

到 2025 年，生态环境质量总体显著改善，沿淮干支流区域生态涵养能力大幅度提高，水资源配置能力和用水效率进一步提高，水功能区水质达标率提高到 95% 以上，形成合理开发、高效利用的水资源开发利用和保护体系；淮河水道基本建成，现代化综合交通运输体系更加完善，基础设施互联互通水平显著提升；现代化经济体系初步形成，优势产业集群不断发展壮大，综合实力和科技创新能力显著增强；以城市群为主体，大中小城市和小城镇协调发展的城镇格局进一步优化，城镇化水平稳步提高；"淮河文化"品牌初步打响，基本公共服务均等化和人民生活水平显著提升；协调统一、运行高效的流域、区域管理体制全面建立，各类要素流动更加通畅，对外开放进一步扩大，内外联动、陆海协同的开放格局初步形成，区域综合实力和竞争力明显提高。

到 2035 年，生态环境根本好转，美丽淮河目标基本实现，经济实力、科技实力大幅提升，人民生活更加宽裕，乡村振兴取得决定性进展，农业农村现代化基本实现，城乡区域发展差距和居民生活水平差距显著缩

through Lianyungang, Suqian, Huai'an, Yancheng, Yangzhou, which is based on the Xinyi-Changxing Railway, Beijing-Shanghai Highway, Beijing-Hangzhou Canal, Lianyungang-Huai'an-Yangzhou-Zhenjiang Expressway under the construction and the second channel of the Beijing-Shanghai Railway under planning; the development axis from Luohe, Zhumadian to Xinyang, which is based on the Beijing-Guangzhou Railway, and the development axis from Heze to Liu'an, passing through Shangqiu, Bozhou and Fuyang, which is based on the Beijing-Kowloon Railway; the development axis from Jining to Chuzhou, passing through Zaozhuang, Xuzhou, Huaibei, Suzhou, Bengbu and Huainan, which is based on the Beijing-Shanghai Railway. Relying on the four development axes, it connects the Yangtze River Delta urban agglomeration, urban agglomeration in the middle reaches of the Yangtze River and Wanjiang urban belt to the south, and to the north connects the Beijing-Tianjin-Hebei region and the Central Plains urban agglomeration, focusing on attracting population and industrial agglomeration, and driving the development of northern Jiangsu, northern Anhui, eastern Henan, southern Shandong and northeastern Hubei.

"Multiple Sites" refer to those cities other than the regional central cities. The development of these cities helps to expand the city's scale and its comprehensive strength, to play the key role of city, to develop industries with distinctive local features and advantages according to local conditions, and to improve the supply of infrastructure and capacity of public services. Development of these cities also helps to attract the migrant agricultural population, strengthen the economic contact and interaction with regional central cities, play a multi-point supporting role in the development of the Huaihe River ecological economic belt, and enhance the driving capacity for the development of the surrounding areas.

4. Prospects

By 2025, the overall ecological and environmental quality will be significantly improved, the ecological conservation capacity of the regions along the trunk stream and tributaries of the Huaihe River will be greatly enhanced, the water resources allocation capacity and water use efficiency will be further enhanced, and the water quality compliance rate of the water functional areas will be raised to over 95 percent, and a water resources system of rational development,

小，产业分工协作格局不断巩固，基本公共服务均等化基本实现，现代社会治理格局基本形成，建成美丽宜居、充满活力、和谐有序的生态经济带，基本实现社会主义现代化。

田铺大塆民俗村（信阳学院冯葆炜摄影）

Tianpu Dawan, a Village Known for Her Unique Folk Custom

(Photography by Feng Baowei, Xinyang University)

efficient utilization and protection will be finally established and formulated. As for transportation, waterways along the Huaihe River will be established, the modern comprehensive transportation system will be further improved and there will be obvious enhancement of sharing with infrastructures of various basins. For the economic system, modern economic system will be initially formulated, and there will be increasing development of competitive industries and obvious development in integral economic capabilities and technological innovation. As to urbanization, the coordinated development pattern between cities and towns will move forward and the standard of urbanization will be steadily enhanced. The brand "Culture Along the Huaihe River" would be initially known to all. Every citizen could enjoy public service and people's living standards will be notably improved. A coordinated, effective regional management system would be fully established in the river basin to ensure the free and unobstructed circulation of all key elements. And a more favorable opening up policy would be put into practice to initially formulate the prospect of intimate and coordinated cooperation both between inland regions and the sea, as well as home and abroad, so as to notably improve the integral capacities and competitiveness of the region.

By 2035, the ecological environment will be fundamentally improved, the goal of beautiful Huaihe River will be basically achieved, and a great leap will be taken in economic, scientific and technological strength. People will be better off, rural revitalization will make decisive progress, and rural modernization will be largely achieved, meaning that the development gap between urban and rural areas, and the gap in living standards will be notably narrowed. Modern social management pattern will basically take shape, a beautiful, livable, dynamic, harmonious and orderly ecological economic belt will be fundamentally built, and socialist modernization will be basically achieved.

二、淮河干流港：淮滨港

1. 淮滨港的前世今生

陈列在信阳市博物馆内的"中华第一舟"，是定位淮河水运的一个远古坐标，讲述着淮滨悠久的航运历史。3500多年前，这艘独木舟搁浅在了淮滨闾河口的淮河岸边，成为悠久岁月的一个见证。

淮滨古称乌龙集，是依托淮河航运兴起的小镇，曾有"南通余杭，北达涿郡"的航运记载。乌龙集处于淮河上游鄂、豫、皖三省交界地，淮河、洪河、白露河互联互通。自古从北面来的粮食，从南面大别山来的山货，从西面来的木材、瓷器、陶器都在乌龙集交易，然后装船运往淮河下游淮南、蚌埠及江苏、上海等地。

淮滨因淮水而兴县，信阳淮滨港——河南省最大的水运港口，自古以来就是豫南地区重要的货物集散地。货物自此东到皖鲁，南至江浙，通江达海，畅通无阻。淮滨因此享有中原地区"出海大通道"的美誉。

2. 淮滨临港经济区的自身优势

（1）适航条件优越

淮河淮滨段拥有地势平坦的淮河岸线资源66公里，县城附近可作港口的岸线近20公里，平均水深4~5米，是整个淮河主干道航运的起点。目前已建成的淮滨饮马港被称为"千里长淮第一港"，港口枯水期水深4~5米，丰水期可达11米，可常年保证1500吨级载重船舶通航，丰水期可通航3000吨级船舶。淮滨航运波及淮河水系、长江水系、京杭运河，直达沿海发达省份。

（2）集疏运条件优越，多式联运格局形成

淮滨县是河南省158个县（市区）中唯一集公路、铁路、水运三种运输方式交汇的县城。两条国道、五条省道在县境内四通八达；四条高

II. The Huaibin Harbour: A Mainstream Harbor of the Huaihe River

1. The Huaibin Harbour---Past and Present

The first canoe of China displayed in Xinyang Museum is an ancient coordinate to locate the water transportation of the Huaihe River, telling the long shipping history of Huaibin. About 3,500 years ago, this canoe ran aground on the banks of the Huaihe River at the estuary of the Lühe River, a testament to the long history.

Huaibin, named as Wulong Bazaar in ancient times, was a small town thriving for its waterways, providing access to Yuhang(present Hangzhou, Zhejiang Province) toward the south and Zhuojun (present Zhuozhou, Hebei Province) County toward the north according to records. Wulong Bazaar was located in the boundary area of Hubei, Henan and Anhui provinces, where the Huaihe River, Honghe River and Bailu River converged together. Since ancient times, grain from the north, mountain goods from the Dabie Mountains in the south, and timber, porcelain and pottery from the west were all collected and traded here in Wulong, and then shipped to Huainan, Bengbu, Jiangsu and Shanghai in the lower reaches of the Huaihe River.

Thanks to the Huaihe River, Huaibin thrived. The Huaibin harbour in Xinyang, which is the biggest shipping port in Henan Province, has been an important goods collection and distribution center in the southern areas of Henan Province since the ancient times. The goods can reach everywhere through the waterways along the Huaihe River. For instance, they can arrive at Anhui and Shandong provinces to the east, and Jiangsu and Zhejiang provinces to the south. Thus, Huaibin is known as "the Big Channel Down to Sea" in central China.

2. The Advantages of the Huaibin Harbor Economic Zone

(1) Favorable Condition of Navigation

The Huaibin section of the Huaihe River has 66 kilometers of shoreline resources with flat land. The bank line near the county seat can be used as a port for nearly 20 kilometers, and the average water depth is 4-5 meters. It is the

速公路(淮息、淮固已建成通车,淮阜高速于2021年开工建设,淮固高速至济广高速连接线正立项审批)连贯南北、承东启西;京九铁路穿境而过,部分路段已开工建设;48公里的淮息航运疏浚工程已开工建设;明港机场、潢川机场、阜阳机场、武汉天河机场均在2小时经济圈内。淮滨临港经济区"公铁水空"综合交通体系完善,其河南出海"南大门"和通江达海"桥头堡"地位突出,是中原经济区融入长江经济带、泛长三角地区的前沿阵地。

位于淮滨县的淮滨港,是历史上著名的水运码头(吴晓军摄影)
Huaibin Harbour, a Historically Well-known Water Transportation Harbour (Photography by Wu Xiaojun)

starting point of the trunk shipping waterway of the Huaihe River. At present, the Yinma harbour in Huaibin County has been established as "the biggest harbour along the Huaihe River". The water depth of the port is 4-5 meters in dry season and 11 meters in wet season, which can ensure the navigability of 1,500-ton heavy-duty ships all year round and 3,000-ton ships in wet season. The waterways in Huaibin County are connected with the waterway along the Huaihe River, the waterway along the Yangtze River, and Beijing-Hangzhou Canal, finally arriving at all the developed coastal provinces.

(2) Favorable Collecting and Distributing Condition and Multi-modal Transportation System

Among the 158 counties in Henan Province, Huaibin County is the only one where highway, railway and waterway converge together. Two national and five provincial highways extend in all directions all over the county. Four highways (Huaibin-Xixian highway and Huaibin-Gushi highway have been built; Huaibin-Fuyang highway started to be built in 2021; and the connection between Huaibin-Gushi highway and Jinan-Guangzhou highway is awaiting approval) combine the south and the north of China, and extend from the east to the west of China. Beijing-Kowloon railway passes through Huaibin County. The 48 km Huaibin-Xixian waterway has begun construction. It takes only two hours from Minggang airport, Huangchuan airport, Fuyang airport or Tianhe airport in Wuhan. The economic zone near Huaibin harbour with the comprehensive transportation system is "the Gateway" from Henan Province to the sea and "the Fortress" for access to all rivers, as well as the frontier for the integration of Central Plains Economic Zone into the Yangtze River Delta, and the pan-Yangtze River Delta.

三、淮河支流港：周口港

1. 周口港的前世今生

周口原称周家口，自明朝始，因漕运而兴，至清代，凭借航运和商贸优势，跻身中原四大名镇。曾几何时，这里舟车辐辏，万商云集，成为北通燕赵、南达江楚、西接秦晋、东连泗河的繁华商埠。"万家灯火侔江浦，千帆云集似汉皋"，明代大学士熊廷弼过周口有感而发，盛赞沙颍河航运商贸的繁荣与兴盛。

周口港现有三条通江达海的通道：第一条通道是从淮河、京杭大运河到长江走南通港，直通大海，共913公里；第二条通道是走淮河，经洪泽湖，通过京杭大运河到淮阴沿河，顺着沿河到达连云港，直通大海，共772公里；第三条通道是走淮安到大丰港，然后直通大海。目前，港口自西向东一字排列有50个停泊船位，年货物吞吐量达4000万吨左右，开通了5条集装箱航线，分别是太仓港、上海港、南通港、连云港、大丰港，打通了与世界航运交流的窗口。

2. 周口临港经济区的自身优势

周口发展临港经济，有地利、天时与人和。

"地利"主要是指周口有得天独厚的地理优势，境内的沙颍河是淮河的最大支流，有2000多年航运历史，曾是著名的鸿沟水系的重要组成部分，是国家规划水运主通道"两横一纵两网十八线"中"一纵"的重要组成部分。沙颍河航道升级改造工程采用4级航道标准，正在积极实施。工程完工后，航道年通过能力将达1.5亿吨，船闸通过能力达到5000万吨以上。尤其是"引江济淮"工程完工后，周口到达长江主航道的航运里程将缩短400公里，届时周口港将成为中原城市群和长三角沟通的水上门户，极大方便了周口同长江中下游地区和武汉城市群之间

III. Zhoukou Harbour: A Branch Harbour of the Huaihe River

1. The Zhoukou Harbour: Past and Present

Zhoukou, originally named Zhoujiakou, has thrived due to grain shipping since the Ming Dynasty. To the Qing Dynasty and thanks to shipping and trade business, Zhoukou was among one of the four famous towns in Central China. It became a prosperous business harbour, with connections to the Yan and Zhao kingdoms in the north, the Chu Kingdom to the south, and the Qin and Jin kingdoms to the west, as well as the Si River to the east. When Xiong Tingbi, a celebrity in the Ming Dynasty, passed through Zhoukou, he sighed with emotion, "A myriad of twinkling lights sparking like those sparking in Pukou, Nanjing; thousands of ships getting together like those assembling in Hankou, Wuhan", which highly implied the prosperous and thriving shipping and trade spectacle on the Shaying River, Zhoukou harbour.

At present, there are three channels of the Zhoukou harbour, providing access to rivers and sea. The first channel passes through the Huaihe River, the Beijing-Hangzhou Grand Canal to the Yangtze River, then to Nantong harbour and finally to the sea. The second channel passes through the Huaihe River, from the Beijing-Hangzhou Grand Canal, the Hongze lake and the Huaiyin harbor to Lianyungang and finally to the sea at 772 kilometers away. The third channel starts from Huai'an to the Dafeng harbour, and finally to the sea. At present, there are 50 anchor positions in line from the west to the east of the harbour. The annual amount of import and export reaches up to 40 million tons and there are five container lines, respectively starting from Taicang harbour, Shanghai harbour, Nantong harbour, Lianyungang harbour and Dafeng harbour, which can trade with other countries all over the world.

2. The Advantages of the Zhoukou Harbour Economic Zone

It is in the right place, at the right time and with the right people for Zhoukou to implement harbour economy.

"In the right place" refers to the favorable geographical advantage of

鸟瞰周口港
A Panoramic View of Zhoukou Harbor

的货运交流；同时助力周口打造"满城文化半城水，内联外通达江海"的中原港城。北上，周口港衔接郑州航空港、郑欧班列、河南自贸试验区，联手打造"公铁水空"多式联运枢纽。南下，周口港加强与淮河、京杭大运河、长江沿线港口互动合作，积极与上海港、南京港、连云港港等沿海大港口对接，实现信息互联互通，形成河河联运、河海联运。

"天时"主要是指周口面临难得的发展机遇，"一带一路"倡议对内河航运提出新需求，新时期开放战略聚焦东部沿海地区的同时，把目光也投向了广阔的中原腹地，河南省委、省政府把支持发展临港经济放在重要位置，写进2018年《政府工作报告》。周口已成功申建为国家级多式联运枢纽试点城市，为发展临港经济带来了机遇、创造了条件。

Zhoukou, richly endowed by nature. The Shaying River in Zhoukou is the biggest branch of the Huaihe River with a shipping history of over 2,000 years. The Shaying River was once a vital part of the famous Honggou hydrographic system and is now a significant part of the main waterway. It is an important "one longitudinal" in the national planning water transport main channel of "two horizontal, one longitudinal, two networks and eighteen lines". The waterway upgrading and reconstructing project of the Shaying River adopts the Level 4 waterway standard and is being actively implemented. Upon completion of the project, the annual passage capacity of the waterway will reach 150 million tons, and the passage capacity of the locks will reach more than 50 million tons. Especially after the completion of the "Water Diversion Project from the Yangtze River to the Huaihe River", the shipping route from Zhoukou to the main waterway of the Yangtze River will be reduced by 400 kilometers, and by then, the Zhoukou harbour will become a water gateway for the communication between the Central Plains urban agglomeration and the Yangtze River Delta, providing a great convenience for the freight shipping between the areas from midstream to downstream of the Yangtze River, and the cities surrounding Wuhan. Zhoukou aims to be forged into a harbour city of the Central Plains, well-known as "with the city culture on waterway, it can connect many cities inside and get access to the sea outside". To the north, the Zhoukou harbour can access the Zhengzhou airport, the Zhengzhou-Europe railway, and the free trade area in Henan Province, becoming a multi-modal transportation hub. To the south, the Zhoukou harbour intensifies the cooperation with the ports along the Huaihe River, the ports along the Beijing-Hangzhou Grand Canal, and the ports along the Yangtze River to reinforce the trade with Shanghai harbour, Nanjing harbour, Lianyungang harbour, etc. Finally, the shipping alliance will come into being.

"At the right time" refers to a unique development opportunity for Zhoukou. The "Belt and Road Initiative" has put forward new demands for inland waterway navigation. While focusing on the eastern coastal areas, the opening strategy in the new era also focuses on the vast hinterland of the Central Plains. The Party Committee and the Government of Henan Province have given priority to supporting the development of the harbour economy, which was written into the *2018 Government Work Report*. Zhoukou has been successfully applied to

今日周口港
Present Zhoukou Harbor

　　"人和"主要是指"2017年临港经济发展论坛"在郑州举行后，郑州又成功举办了"2018年临港经济高峰论坛"，周口市不仅拿出了方法论，画出了路线图，而且现场得到专家献智、企业签约，踏上了快车道，合作签约丰硕，与临港经济有关的35个项目签约，总投资达577.2亿元。

be the National Multi-modal Transportation Hub Pilot City, which has brought opportunities and created conditions for the development of harbour economy.

"With the right people" mainly refers to the strong intellectual support from and close contact with many companies. After the "2017 Forum on Harbour Economy Development" held in Zhengzhou, Zhoukou not only prepared the development pattern and the route design of waterway, but also received guidance from many experts and signed contracts with many companies in the "2018 Summit on Harbour Economy Development", which was also held in Zhengzhou. At this forum, Zhoukou signed 35 contracts concerning the harbour economy development, and the total investment amounted to 57.72 billion *yuan*.

四、淮河边走出的外交官：苟皓东

1. 把最好的年华献给"一带一路"

苟皓东，1960年生，资深外交官，中国公共外交协会会员、中国非洲研究院特约研究员。先后就读于淮滨县高级中学、广州外国语学院（现广东外语外贸大学）、外交学院国际法专业。曾任中国驻非盟使团副代表、中国驻坦桑尼亚大使馆公使衔参赞、中国驻印度尼西亚登巴萨总领事等职务，在中国驻澳大利亚、伊朗、厄立特里亚、利比里亚、博茨瓦纳、坦桑尼亚、埃塞俄比亚、印度尼西亚等"一带一路"沿线国家的外交机构工作长达20余年，对国外政治、经济、社会、文化、宗教等方面具有深入的观察和思考，曾在《世界博览》《环球》《中国青年报》《大公报》等刊物发表游记和政论文章。

2. 因为了解所以热爱

"非洲人总体上质朴、善良、乐观、正直、热情。"苟皓东说。非洲人和中国人在价值观，甚至思维方式上有很多相似之处，比如，重亲情，讲人情，利他，分享，等等。"我第一次常驻的非洲国家是厄立特里亚，伊萨亚斯总统对我们说过这么一句话：'我从内心深处和中国人有一种天然的亲切感。'我在这个非洲国家工作了五年，交了许多朋友。五年里，我走遍了厄立特里亚的全部省区，到过大部分城镇和无数个村落，最远的行程五天四夜，沿途搭帐篷过夜或投宿荒村，很多次遇到困难和危险，总有好心人相助。离开厄立特里亚的前一周，我最后一次长途出差，空军司令为我们一行派了总统座机。河床、沙漠、戈壁、高山、峡谷一掠而过，我辨认出很多地方，飞行员惊讶不已。直升飞机到了首都阿斯马拉的上空，我请飞行员盘旋一周。俯瞰着暮色里每一个熟悉的角落，心里很不是滋味。"

IV. Gou Haodong: A Diplomat Having Grown Up by the Huaihe River

1. Dedication of His Best Years to "the Belt and Road Initiative"

Gou Haodong, born in 1960, is an experienced diplomat, a member of China Public Diplomacy Association, and guest researcher of China Institute of African Studies. He successively studied in Huaibin Senior High School, Guangzhou Institute of Foreign Language (present Guangdong University of Foreign Studies), and China Foreign Affairs University, majoring in International Law. He once was the A. U. mission deputy representative, the Chinese embassy in Tanzania minister counsellor, the consul general of China in Denpasar, Indonesia. He has worked for more than 20 years in the countries along the "Belt and Road" such as Australia, Iran, Eritrea, Liberia, Botswana, Tanzania, Ethiopia and Indonesia, etc., gaining profound insight and thought on foreign politics, economics, society, culture and religion. Some of his travelogues and political essays were published in periodicals like *World Vision*, *Globe*, *China Youth Daily*, *Takungpao*, etc.

2. Devotion Because of Understanding

Gou Haodong was convinced that the Africans, generally speaking, are simple, kind, optimistic, upright and passionate. There are many similarities in values, even in the ways of thinking between the Africans and the Chinese, such as valuing the importance of family affection, the importance of human relationship, altruism, sharing, etc. "The African country where I worked for the first time was Eritrea. The president Assayas had said to us, 'There is natural intimacy with Chinese people deep in my heart.' I worked in this country for five years and made many friends. In these five years, I travelled all the provinces and regions in Eritrea, and went to most towns and countless villages. The farthest journey lasted five days and four nights. In this journey, I pitched a tent or stayed in deserted village. I encountered many difficulties and dangerous things but there were always many good-hearted people to help me. During the last week before leaving Eritrea, I took my last long-distance business trip. The air force commander provided us with the president's airplane. The pilot was surprised at

非洲老百姓大多数安贫乐道,讲礼貌,守秩序。到过埃塞俄比亚的中国朋友估计都见过当地人等车排队,经常是队伍排成几百米,没有人拥挤争抢上车。有一次在山路上,苟皓东遇到两个卖劈柴的妇女,背着足足上百斤的劈柴蹒跚下山。他上去与其中一个妇女攀谈,了解到她从天不亮上山砍柴,再到山下卖柴,大半天才能挣到相当于人民币十多元钱。他给她拍照后给了一点小费,她立即转身分给了她身后的另外一个妇女。

3. 夫妇协力以苦为乐

苟皓东和夫人
Gou Haodong and His Wife

苟皓东在非洲工作的大多数时间里,妻子孙丽华也被从高校借调到大使馆工作,在外交活动中给予了苟皓东很大的支持和协助。孙丽华还在业余时间教当地人学汉语,同时向当地人学习非洲语言,先后学习了

my recognizing many places as riverbed, desert, Gobi, mountains, and canyon as we flew away. When the airplane reached the capital Asmara, I begged the pilot to circle. I felt grieved at the sight of every familiar corner in the dusk."

Most of people in Africa always feel happy even though they are poor. They are polite and law-abiding. The Chinese who have been to Ethiopia have seen the local people in Ethiopia waiting for the bus in line. Even though they line up for hundreds of meters, there is no crowding and nobody scrambles for the bus. Gou Haodong once met two women on a mountain road who went to sell firewood. They stumbled down the mountain with more than 50 kilograms of firewood on their back. Gou Haodong talked with one of them and learned that she cut the firewood before dawn, went down the mountain and sold it, and earned no more than 10 RMB a day. He gave some tips after taking a photo of her, while she shared immediately the tips with the other woman.

3. Sharing Weal and Woe Together

Most of the time when Gou Haodong worked in Africa, his wife, Sun Lihua as a university teacher, was sent to work in the embassy with him and offered great support and assistance in diplomatic activities. In her spare time, Sun Lihua taught Chinese to the local people and learned the African languages such as Eritrea Ertra, Amharic language, and Swahili. She also researched African culture and published two volumes on *African Tribal Cultures* with some other teachers.

"In Liberia, I got a vaccination of malaria every year. The first three years in Liberia, the housing conditions in the embassy were very poor. Without the power supply from municipal administration, we got power from an electric generator, which made noise. We dug a well to drink some water. Sometimes I felt disappointed, but never gave in. I was encouraged by my wife's companionship in such rough times. Her passion for Africa encouraged me the most. It is well-known that she has great language talent, but I was amazed by her motivation in learning African languages." said Gou Haodong.

A young colleague appraised Gou Haodong, "Counselor Gou is such a person that he devoted most of his life to diplomatic affairs, full of passion on life and strong affections to Africa. Even in such a rough time, he always worked full of passion. With popular diplomatic words, Gou Haodong is a person with a

提格雷尼亚语、阿姆哈拉语、斯瓦西里语,研究非洲文化,挤出时间与几位高校教师撰写出版了两辑《非洲部族文化纵览》。

"在利比里亚,我每年都打疟疾,到利比里亚最初那两三年,使馆住房条件很差,没有市政供电,用电全靠发电机,震耳欲聋,饮用水靠自己打井。也暗自沮丧过,但没有趴下。那样的苦日子,妻子的陪伴给了我很大的鼓励。她对我更大的鼓励是她对非洲的热爱和好奇。大家都说她有语言天赋,只有我知道,她学习非洲语言的动力来自何处。"

一位年轻同事曾撰文这样评价他:"苟参赞就是这样一个人,他大半辈子投身于外交事业,对生活充满了热爱和情趣,对非洲更是有着浓厚的感情,哪怕在如此艰苦的地方工作都始终饱含激情,用现在流行的外交语来说,是一个爱外交、会生活的人。他喜欢和年轻人打成一片,和他在使馆里工作过的年轻人也都喜欢和他相处,他对生活的乐观、对工作的热情深深地感染着每个年轻人,逐渐成了他们工作和生活中的良师益友。"

passion for diplomacy and for life. He liked to be friends with young people and got on well with the young colleagues in the embassy. His optimism in life, and his passion for work deeply influenced every young colleague and they gradually became friends for life."

结 语

淮河文化因创造中华文化大融合、大发展的高峰而光彩夺目，也因谱写战天斗地的治淮史诗而催人奋进。

淮河文化涵盖了包括民为邦本的民本文化、不屈不挠的奋斗文化、公平正义的法治文化、顾全大局的奋斗文化、敢为人先的改革文化、兼收并蓄的开放文化在内的中华优秀传统文化的精髓，淮河文化穿越时空，闪耀着人文光辉，为新时代国家制度和治理体系建设、全面依法治国、改革开放提供了有力的借鉴和强大的支撑。

习近平总书记指出，要加强对中华优秀传统文化的挖掘和阐发，使中华民族最基本的文化基因与当代文化相适应、与现代社会相协调，把跨越时空、超越国界、富有永恒魅力、具有当代价值的文化精神弘扬起来。今天，我们开展淮河文化的研究与传播，必须坚持"创造性转化、创新性发展"，把淮河文化的当代价值发掘和提炼好、宣传和运用好，让淮河文化在新时代焕发生机活力、发挥独特作用。

Conclusion

The Huaihe River culture sparks with dazzling brilliance for her bringing about the great integration and development of Chinese culture, and inspiring people because of the composition of the epic to tame the Huaihe River as well.

The Huaihe River culture bears the quintessence of the outstanding traditional culture of the Chinese nation, including: people-oriented culture ensuring the fundamental position of civilians in the nation, striving culture characterizing with tenacity and perseverance, law-based culture highlighting fairness and justice, reform culture proposing innovation and initiation, and opening-up culture advocating all-embracing temperament. The Huaihe River culture, traversing time and space and glowing with humanistic splendor, provides powerful reference and strong support in the New Era for the construction of state and administrative systems, as well as for comprehensively governing of the country by law, practicing reform and opening up policy.

General Secretary Xi Jinping pinpoints the fact that it is necessary to reinforce the exploration and interpretation of splendid traditional Chinese culture, and manage to fulfill the adaption and coordination between the most basic cultural gene of the Chinese nation and contemporary culture and society, so as to carry forward the cultural spirit that transcends boundaries of nation, with eternal charm and contemporary value. At present, we must uphold the notion of "creative transformation and innovative development" when carrying out the research and dissemination of the Huaihe River culture. We must manage to perfectly explore, refine, disseminate and utilize the contemporary value of the Huaihe River culture, and exert the vitality and unique role of the Huaihe River culture in the New Era.

附录：中国历史年代简表

Appendix: A Brief Chronology of Chinese History

中国历史年代简表

A Brief Chronology of Chinese History

五帝时代 Period of the Five Legendary Rulers c. 2600 BC-c. 2070 BC	黄帝 Huangdi (Yellow Emperor)	
	颛顼 Zhuanxu	
	帝喾 Diku (Emperor Ku)	
	尧 Yao	
	舜 Shun	
夏 Xia Dynasty	c. 2070 BC-c. 1600 BC	
商 Shang Dynasty	c. 1600 BC-c. 1046 BC	
西周 Western Zhou Dynasty	c. 1046 BC-c. 771 BC	
东周 Eastern Zhou Dynasty 770 BC-256 BC	春秋 Spring and Autumn Period	770 BC-476 BC
	战国 Warring States Period	475 BC-221 BC
秦 Qin Dynasty	221 BC-206 BC	
汉 Han Dynasty 206 BC-220 AD	西汉 Western Han	206 BC-25 AD
	东汉 Eastern Han	25 AD-220 AD
三国 Three Kingdoms 220 AD-280 AD	魏 Wei	220 AD-265 AD
	蜀汉 Shu Han	221 AD-263 AD
	吴 Wu	222 AD-280 AD
晋 Jin Dynasty 265 AD-420 AD	西晋 Western Jin	265 AD-317 AD
	东晋 Eastern Jin	317 AD-420 AD

续表 Continued Table

南北朝 Southern and Northern Dynasties 420 AD-589 AD	南朝 Southern Dynasties	宋 Song	420 AD-479 AD
		齐 Qi	479 AD-502 AD
		梁 Liang	502 AD-557 AD
		陈 Chen	557 AD-589 AD
	北朝 Northern Dynasties	北魏 Northern Wei	386 AD-534 AD
		东魏 Eastern Wei	534 AD-550 AD
		北齐 Northern Qi	550 AD-577 AD
		西魏 Western Wei	535 AD-556 AD
		北周 Northern Zhou	557 AD-581 AD
隋 Sui Dynasty		581 AD-618 AD	
唐 Tang Dynasty		618 AD-907 AD	
五代十国 Five Dynasties and Ten States	五代 Five Dynasties 907 AD-960 AD	后梁 Later Liang	907 AD-923 AD
		后唐 Later Tang	923 AD-936 AD
		后晋 Later Jin	936 AD-947 AD
		后汉 Later Han	947 AD-950 AD
		后周 Later Zhou	951 AD-960 AD
	十国 Ten States 902 AD-979 AD	北汉 Northern Han	951 AD-979 AD
		吴 Wu	902 AD-937 AD
		吴越 Wuyue	907 AD-978 AD
		闽 Min	909 AD-945 AD
		南汉 Southern Han	917 AD-971 AD
		荆南（又称"南平"）Jingnan (Nanping)	924 AD-963 AD
		楚 Chu	927 AD-951 AD
		南唐 Southern Tang	937 AD-975 AD
		前蜀 Former Shu	907 AD-925 AD
		后蜀 Later Shu	934 AD-965 AD

续表 Continued Table

宋 Song Dynasty 960 AD-1279 AD	北宋 Northern Song	960 AD-1127 AD
	南宋 Southern Song	1127 AD-1279 AD
辽 Liao (契丹 Qidan/Khitan)	907 AD-1125 AD	
西夏 Xixia (Tangut)	1038 AD-1227 AD	
金 Jin	1115 AD-1234 AD	
元 Yuan Dynasty	1206 AD-1368 AD	
明 Ming Dynasty	1368 AD-1644 AD	
清 Qing Dynasty	1616 AD-1911 AD	
中华民国 Republic of China	1912 AD-1949 AD	
中华人民共和国 People's Republic of China	1949 AD-	